Strangers in the Night

Mentally Ill Mothers and Their Effects on Their Children

Nelly Maseda, MD

iUniverse, Inc.
Bloomington

Strangers in the Night
Mentally Ill Mothers and Their Effects on Their Children

iUniverse books may be ordered through booksellers or by contacting:

iUniverse
1663 Liberty Drive
Bloomington, IN 47403
www.iuniverse.com
1-800-Authors (1-800-288-4677)

ISBN: 978-1-4759-4272-9 (sc)
ISBN: 978-1-4759-4273-6 (hc)
ISBN: 978-1-4759-4388-7 (ebk)

Printed in the United States of America

iUniverse rev. date: 09/22/2012

For My Two Cupie Dolls,
Sarah and Matthew
You Heal Me

Contents

Introduction

There is a question I have been asked over and over again whose answer eludes and haunts me. It is "Why did you 'make it' and not your brothers?" It is a question often posed by my educated friends who, with every good intention, are curious about those of us—in my case, someone raised by a single Dominican mother on public assistance—who made it into the classrooms of a prestigious institution of higher education. While I was pursuing my degree at Cornell University, my brothers and cousins entered into a world of substance abuse and its related criminal activities and violence. Anger characterized much of our mental states. The difference is that for me, anger was an energizer to achieve academically. Reading and learning were coping mechanisms to escape the chaos around me.

During a review session for my chemistry class during my freshman year in college, our teaching assistant stopped for a moment while solving equations on the blackboard to look at us and say, "I know how frustrating this is, but I want you to use your anger at not understanding this material to say to yourself, 'I am going to get this.'" I thought to myself at that instant, *She just described what I have been doing for most of my life.* I did not know it as a child, and as a teenager, there was not a label to describe my drive to get straight As and my desire to focus on my future and get out of my situation at home. I turned away from that evil and looked at something better. Learning was not just something I loved engaging my mind in, but also my therapy, a positive channel for anger.

And so it is with this in mind that I want to try to answer that extremely loaded and complicated question. I wrote this book with the intended audience being the beautiful patients I have had the privilege to serve as a pediatrician for in the Bronx, some of whom lead lives very much like mine was as a child, with violence in the home. They are children with the seed of rage implanted in them.

In the first vignettes, I describe the life of my mother, Nena, as told to me by her and her siblings, who were born and raised in the Dominican Republic. Like most immigrants, her main reason for coming to this country in 1959 was better economic prospects. In Nena's case, however, it was not only upward mobility financially that motivated her, but also the desire to escape a dictatorship that brutalized its people and made life especially terrifying for women. I go over some details of her life to share a small amount of the history of this island. I also hope to show how Nena thought she left her sadness behind and became renewed in New York City when she found love in her new country, as well as the mental deterioration that followed once she lost what she believed was the key to her happiness, left alone with children to raise after my father abandoned us.

So many people in our country, political leaders included, will voice opposition to using government funds that will help children by stating, "It is not the government's job to . . . it's the parent's job." But what if you don't have parents? What if you don't have functional parents? What if your parents are not able to provide an environment where young, vulnerable minds can be nurtured? What of children who do not see, in their homes, conduct by their parents that would lead to the positive behaviors we just "expect" everyone to have? What if they are instead exposed to irresponsible sexual behavior, drug use, senseless violence, and demeaning emotional abuse? If these are the acts being modeled in front of innocent and susceptible young children, how do we as a society benefit by ignoring their needs?

Let's take, for example, the children in foster care. Legally, these children have already seen and experienced evil—sometimes of unspeakable proportions. Would it not be to our collective advantage to have them receive the best educational experience that money can buy? With intensive psychiatric support and affectionate caretakers, these young minds can be turned away from the abyss they have stared at, thus preventing them from becoming the evil that too many abused children, unfortunately, become. They are usually placed in communities marked by poverty with families that have few resources. They end up going to low-performing public schools, and many of them are placed in multiple homes. These are all seeds that breed the destructive behaviors I talk about in this book.

The denial in looking away from these souls is too costly. The suffering that they experience, and that those around them experience, is immeasurable. But the actual price tag in dollars is also unacceptably high. In what has been termed the "Pipeline to Prison," foster care children are overrepresented in our prison system. At a cost that can go as high as $217,000 per incarcerated juvenile per year in New York State, doesn't it make sense that we (the collective taxpayer "we") practice prevention of this obscene and immoral Pipeline?

Important as this issue is politically, I am writing about the other side of this equation. On behalf of children who live in homes where they experience fear, I am passionate about convincing parents to accept mental health-care services when needed so that the precious gift of our next generation does not carry the scars of abuse into their adulthood. We, Latinos, people of color, have to unburden ourselves from the obstacles we create by entering into treatment to tame behaviors within us that are harming our children. Let us end the taboo many of us have against accepting mental health-care services. There is no shame in receiving mental health treatment.

It is only a shame when we need it but don't seek it or accept it.

This book aims to look inside the dynamics of a family in which the mother has severe mood swings, rage, promiscuous sexual behavior, and cycles of depression. I am writing about my mother. Perhaps my "coming out" with this truth of mine will help others see that while no two stories are the same, and no two paths identical, we are now living in a time where help exists to undo the damage that negative, early life experiences can do to our minds and our lives.

October 11, 2003

On a warm October Saturday in New York City, my thirteen-year-old daughter, Sarah, and I are on our way to celebrate the first birthday of my friend's daughter. The venue is an Indian restaurant where long tables are set up with balloons and flowers marking the festive occasion. Each placemat has a chronology of Elisa's first year of life. With the exception of another toddler and Sarah, all present are adults.

About one hour into the gathering, my mother, Nena, walks in. She has her short hair attractively done, button earrings with a matching necklace, and she's wearing a short-sleeved white linen pantsuit. She accompanies Elisa's babysitter, Maria. Nena has been invited because she recommended Maria for this job. Elisa's parents are therefore grateful to my mother. They love Maria, who has become part of their family.

As the gathering progresses, groups have broken off into their small, pleasant conversations, Elisa's grandparents have crowded Maria, and all seem content, except my mother. She has a look on her face that seems to say "look at me." No one is paying attention to her. I try to include her in my conversation, but she looks away. After a few moments and with no relevance to the current conversation, Nena decides to start making fun of me and my suburban life.

"When I go up there to cook for her parties, those white people lick their lips with the *sasón* I add to my food." She has everyone laughing as she gestures and imitates how others respond to her Dominican cooking. She becomes animated as the party progresses, now that she's making people laugh.

The birthday party comes to an end. Sarah and I kiss my mother good-bye.

Nena asks, "What are you going to do now?"

"Sarah and I are going to see a movie at a theatre on Forty-Second Street and Eighth Avenue," I answer.

"Times Square. I'll come with you."

"I don't think you'll enjoy this movie."

"Why?"

"It's about a thirteen-year-old girl who develops a drug habit, drops out of school—"

"I don't care what the movie is about," she interrupts me. "I'll join you just to give me something to do."

The three of us ride the subway downtown. As we're exiting up the stairs toward the street, my mother starts yelling, "*Ahí no hay teatro* [There are no movie theatres here]!"

"Mom, I looked up the theatre location and the times the movie's playing so we could go see it after the party."

"You call that a party? What the hell was that? Dry chicken in an Indian restaurant for a one-year-old? *Jesús, esa comida ni me bajaba, y mira que traté.* [I tried, but I just couldn't swallow that food.] Disgusting trying to eat that. I'm telling you there is no movie theatre here." She is starting to yell.

One constant since Nena arrived in New York City in 1959 are the movie theatres in Times Square, despite the dramatic changes in the area over the past decades. The scene is becoming disturbing. We are in front of the Madame Tussauds Museum. The street is so crowded that people are rubbing past each other as they walk. Nena has slowed her pace. I look back at her. Her arms are up over her head, hairdo undone, and she is screaming, "*Ahí no hay teatros* [There are no movie theatres here]!"

I am unsettled by what is happening. I walk toward Nena, but my daughter grabs my arm and begs, "Mommy, let's just keep walking. She's just being Yaya again."

As I walk ahead, I occasionally look back at her. She's looking disoriented, angry, working up to a rage. With the exception of some tourists whose attention turns to the rant in Spanish, most people ignore her. This is, after all, Times Square.

Sarah and I enter the theatre. Nena follows us in but remains standing by the front door, her hands clasped together, twirling her thumbs, not saying a word. I am really angry at this point. I should be used to her psycho-breaks, but what is really making me furious is that I don't want my daughter to witness this one. I want to grab Nena by the lapel of her linen jacket, shake her until those button earrings fly off, and tell her, "Not in front of my children." However, I control myself and ask her, "Well, now that you see there is a movie theatre here, do you want to see the movie?"

"I'm hungry. I told you I couldn't swallow that dried-up chicken. I need to eat. This movie theatre must have just been put here."

"Mom, do I buy you a ticket for the movie?"

"Well, okay. Now that I'm here, I might as well, *but I need to eat!*" she yells at me.

We buy the tickets, stop at the concessions stand, and after meticulously reviewing the neon menu and making the teenage cashier clarify every item for sale, she settles on popcorn and a bottle of water. When Nena sees me pay, she leans over the counter and yells at the cashier taking my money, "What? A dollar fifty for a bottle of water? What's wrong with you people? Nelita, return the water."

I quietly tell the cashier to take the money and gesture to him, "Never mind the lunatic."

Nena continues with her rapid, pressured speech. "This popcorn is too salty. What's this about a movie about a thirteen-year-old drug addict and a girl? Please, *le doy esa golpía hasta que le rompa hasta el hígado* [I'd beat her so badly, I'd even break her liver] . . . Why so many escalators to get to the theatre? What is this—a journey to the earth's anal opening? To hell with the movie. I'm too tired after all these escalators. Nelita, what were you thinking bringing me here?" And on and on she goes nonstop.

We are finally at our compartmentalized theatre, which has only about five other people in it. Nena sits in front of an elderly woman who has a walker; I sit between Nena and Sarah. I want to make sure Sarah doesn't hear what is sure to be my mother's nonstop verbal assaults. The elderly lady is leaning on her walker, which delivers occasional taps to the back of Nena's seat. The movie hasn't yet started when Nena turns around abruptly and yells.

"Stop tapping on my seat!" She startles the woman.

"Mom, let's move. The theatre is almost empty."

"I'm not the one who has to move; she's the one who has to move," she says, looking behind her.

The movie ends.

"Thank God!" Nena raises her arms and shakes them toward the ceiling. "The movie ended just before my head exploded from that lady's walker tapping," she says, making sure the woman and her aide hear her. "And that mother in the movie, what the hell was she thinking bringing boyfriends into the home with a teenage daughter there? And that daughter, I'll tell you what, if she were my child, *le entro a pata, mira, que hasta el alma se la rompo* [I'd start kicking her until I break even her soul]."

"Mom, I need to run so that I can catch the next train from Grand Central," I say as I kiss her good-bye.

"*Esa es tu escusa* [That's your excuse]?" She squints one eye and points her finger at me. "Don't use the train as an excuse. If you don't want to be with me, just say so."

I'm feeling the rage now. It's contagious, and she can really play with my head. I take a deep breath and remember the emotional distance I've worked so hard to maintain. Going down the set of escalators seems to take hours, and Nena is ranting nonstop.

"*Uno pare y cria para que un dia tus hijos te den una pata y fuera* [You have children and raise them, just to have them kick you out of their lives one day]. I gave you your life, I made you who you are today, and now look at you—you think you're better than me." With her loud voice, she continues down the escalators.

"*Callate ya!* Just shut up!" I cannot believe I'm screaming. We are now outside.

Sarah moves back, and Nena stands still quietly, looking very matter of fact. I see people coming toward us. A crowd has formed around us.

"Why can't I enjoy an afternoon at the movies with you? Why can't we have a simple conversation? Why the accusations, put downs, screaming, drama? You know the movie theatres are here . . . I try to please you . . . Why did you come? Just to abuse me in front of my daughter? Will I ever have a normal day with you?"

I'm trembling with fury, and my throat hurts from screaming when I realize the possibility that in the crowd watching this show we're giving could be a patient of mine or a colleague. I stop my attack on what, to others, must seem like a defenseless, gray-haired, little, old lady. She looks satisfied and walks away.

As Sarah and I ride the train home, I apologize to her for having lost control. I tell my daughter how awful seeing me being abusive toward my mother must have been for her. To create such a scene is inexcusable. We laugh when I say, "I can't believe I became my mother."

I never should have gone out with Nena and then to see a movie with a mother in it who was very much like Nena in her younger days. I need to stop blaming myself. I promise my daughter I will never again put myself in a position to lose control in this way. Sarah is very patient and understanding. I know right now she is feeling sorry for me. Although I hate having my child pity me, I'm also feeling sorry for myself. When will Nena stick with psychiatric treatment?

I think now of why Pepin spends years between having Nena visit him in Miami.

"Peps, are you inviting Mom to come down this Christmas?" I asked him during a recent phone conversation.

"Nelly, I can't have Mom over now. I have guns in the house," he replies.

I laughed when I first heard him say this. Right now, however, I know exactly how he feels.

San Juan de la Maguana

"*Yo vengo de un pueblito, San Juan de la Maguana*[I come from a small town, San Juan de le Maguana]," is Nena's answer when asked what part of the Dominican Republic she is from. This *pueblito* is located on the southwest corner of the country, bordering Haiti. It is easy to accidentally drive into Haiti while there. In 1937, when Nelia Altagracia Rodriguez (Nena) was born there, it had no paved roads, no televisions, and no indoor plumbing. The year 1937 was also when the supreme leader of this tiny country of several million people, Raphael Trujillo, led the Parsley Massacre, a campaign that left thousands of Haitians dead.

The *pueblito* had a church with a priest from Spain, a schoolhouse open to the few who could afford paper and pencil, many tin-roofed shacks, and a few cinderblock homes. The method of transportation was walking or by horse. The local river was shared by the Haitians, who were distinguished by the patois they spoke and their inability to pronounce certain words in Spanish. For example, the word for parsley, *pe-re-jil,* is pronounced "*pe-l-ejil*" by

Haitians, hence the name of the massacre. While being hunted, their pronunciation of this word was a method to distinguish them from the Spanish-speaking Dominicans. For most of the people of San Juan, however, living with the Haitians was uneventful, even though the two governments that shared the island were enemies.

Nena's mother, Ana Santana, lived in a one-room shack with a tin roof. It had no plumbing and no electricity. Ana never learned how to read or write. She ironed clothes for the local police. She was one of those women of the third world who could balance several pounds of groceries on her head to free her hands for more carrying. Her thick, black hair was always pulled back into a bun, and she had green eyes and *café au lait* skin.

Leonte Rodriguez, Nena's father, in contrast came from a well-to-do family with the means to send him to New York to study when he was young. He was a businessman from another town, Santiago. Tall, handsome, intelligent, and known to have a fierce temper, he feared no one. He unleashed his fury and beat on anyone who disrespected him.

Leonte visited his businesses throughout the country and commanded the same fear and respect from those he encountered, the same way his hero, Trujillo, inspected every corner of the island and unleashed reprimands and beatings to the citizenry. The country was on a path set forth by the dictator to Europeanize the Dominicans in their physical characteristics and to teach them proper manners and etiquette [*etiqueta y protocolo*]. On an unannounced visit to any part of the country, Trujillo could surprise anyone, as he was never above challenging a man to a good fist fight for something as minor as wearing an un-ironed shirt or for walking barefoot in public. So, too, Leonte treated his employees, by disciplining them if they behaved in the uncivilized ways the country was now on a mission to abandon. "*El mundo tiene que ver que no somos unos campesinos* [The world needs to see we are not hillbillies]," was one of Leonte's refrains.

To achieve his goal of ridding his country of what he felt were undesirables, Trujillo's genocide against the Haitians extended to the mistreatment of dark-skinned Dominicans, especially those who were not educated. Many Dominicans alive during Trujillo's time said he had an obsession with wanting to be white and was reputed to bathe in bleach to lighten his mulatto skin. Furthermore, to "purify" the race, he gladly accepted European refugees. He welcomed them to this poor, underdeveloped nation while they were being persecuted in the well-known and well-documented genocides occurring in Europe at this time. Nena and her siblings tell me that Trujillo wanted these refugees because they were white and because he hoped that as educated people, they would help develop the island.

In the midst of an island with crippling poverty, people hating their own blackness, and a murderous dictator, Leonte received his firstborn child as a result of his affair with Ana. Nena became the love of Leonte's life. She was beautiful, full of laughter, intelligent, and showed abundant affection toward her Papi. In a country focused on a program of racial purification, Nena was destined to be saved, as she inherited no African features. Leonte thought to himself, *She doesn't have my coarse hair. She doesn't have her mother's broad nose.* "*No hay nada en el mundo mas precioso que mi Nenita* [There is nothing in this world more precious than my little Nena]," Leonte often said. She remained his favorite child for his entire life.

Leonte went on to father seven more children, eight children by three different women in total. His legitimate wife was Leda Alcantara, who accepted all of Leonte's offspring. Leonte was unusual in wanting to keep all of his children together. He was a strict disciplinarian and a good provider. As for the three different mothers, theirs was an amicable relationship. "*Somos como hermanas* [We're like sisters]," is how they described their communal cooperation in raising their children. Mama was basically a maid and was so grateful that Nena was not left behind by her father to live the way so many children of the Dominican Republic do. Begging in the streets for food and money would have been Nena's destiny if raised by her mother alone.

As Nena grew older, Leonte treated her as his prize to show off to his business associates. She accompanied him on his many business trips throughout the island, and when back home, he made all of the younger siblings respect her for her status as the oldest and, according to Leonte, the wisest among his children. Her illegitimacy was never an issue.

Even before she was a teenager, Leonte had already decided Nena would be the one acknowledged at his funeral by receiving the Masonic apron marking her as his heir.

Leonte was a member of the Masons, an unusual status symbol to have in that country at that time. Masons have a tradition in which the apron given to them upon acceptance to the brotherhood is passed on to someone whom they love and whom they feel is worthy of such a possession when they die. The person designated to receive the Masonic apron is considered to symbolize all of the leadership qualities that this group values. Though it is an honor usually passed on to males, Leonte overlooked his sons when he made his decision.

Being a father who adored her in this way, Leonte made sure Nena did not suffer the abject poverty so many Dominicans lived under. She was never comfortable with the economic divide, the inhumanity, the cruelty toward the poor.

Her biological mother lived among the poorest. This fact caused emotional pain for Nena, who tried not to compare her life of comfort to the one she experienced when she visited her mama. When she slept with Mama, she always held the petite eighty-pound woman tightly and with all the love she had to give. She felt she could not do enough to alleviate Mama's poverty, bringing her food, shoes, old clothing, and the pittance she could extract from her father he knew would go to Mama. "*Era tan Buena, tan bondadosa todos la quierrian. Siento ese dolor tan fuerte en verla en esa esclavitud* [She was so good, so charitable. The pain I always felt was deep, watching her work as a slave]." Nena gets emotional when she remembers those days when Mama would smile and distribute these goods to her neighbors.

Back home with Leonte, *etiquetta y protocolo*, how to maintain yourself and your household with the correct appearance "society" expected, is what Nena had to concern herself with. Learning French, which fork to use for salad, and how to set a proper table were lessons Nena gladly participated in to please her Papi. Interfering thoughts of Mama made sure Nena was never too comfortable, never fully accepting that these lessons were really as important as saving Mama from the country's cruel treatment of its poor. Her mind sometimes drifted at such times to the little shack in which Mama lived.

She pictured Mama barefoot on the dirt floor and smelled the coal burning inside the metal container used to heat the iron for the endless loads of laundry Mama had to press. Nena regularly went for fittings to update her wardrobe with new dresses while Mama always seemed to wear the same rags. The country wanted to annihilate people like Mama and the desperately poor children of her neighborhood. People with Nena's beauty were the "face" of Dominicans that Trujillo wanted to show the world.

Nena could not reconcile within herself these two dichotomies.

Nena y Pirulo

A very handsome, young man in a foreign military uniform approached the crowd of teens that was hanging out in el *Parque Colon.* "*Y quien sera esa estrella de cine* [Who might that movie star be]?" Nena asked out loud. "*El Principe Juan Carlos de Bourbon me ha mandado a invitarles a conocerlo en ese barco* [The prince of Spain has sent me to invite you to that ship to meet him]," the man in the uniform answered as he pointed to a docked yacht. The prince of Spain was touring Latin American countries and at each stop wanted to meet as many Spanish-speaking citizens as he could. The Spaniards in turn were treated to a close look at the natives of the new world.

With a mixture of excitement and disbelief, this young crowd of boys and girls followed the cadet into the yacht named *Juan Sebastian el Cano*. On board, live music was playing, and food was served, allowing the visiting Spanish military men to have a social interchange with local Dominicans. "*Que hombres mas bello* [What beautiful men]," Nena and her friends whispered to each other as they admired, danced with, and flirted with the young cadets. El Principe Juan Carlos danced with each young lady for a few minutes to give her a memory to relish for a lifetime.

Some Dominican military men were socializing as well. One of them, Gilberto Sanchez Rubirosa (a.k.a. Pirulo), had his eyes set on Nena. "*Mientras yo perseguia a los Espanoles, Pirulo me perseguia a mi* [While I chased the young Spaniards, Pirulo chased me]." El Coronel Gilberto Sanchez Rubirosa courted Nena until she became his common-law wife when she was just fourteen years old.

Pirulo's parents were Ana Rubirosa, who had been a model in Paris, and his father, Gilberto Sanchez Lustrino, a well-known Dominican author and part of the Dominican delegation in France. Ana's brother, Porfirio Rubirosa, Pirulo's uncle, was a notorious international playboy romantically linked to Hollywood celebrities, such as Zsa Zsa Gabor, and married to Barbara Hutton.

In keeping with Trujillo's campaign to Europeanize the Dominican Republic, he sought to import white émigrés. When he lived in Europe in the 1930s and 1940s, Trujillo had Porfirio Rubirosa help Jews obtain safe passage to the island, hoping to infuse his country with their "superior" genes. Pirulo himself was trained for military duty in the United States (at West Point, or so Nena claims).

To be in the company of people from such high culture and power was exactly what Leonte had made Nena believe was her destiny (though Nena never described how she felt about having to perform her duties for Pirulo). Ana Rubirosa taught Nelia Rodriguez how to carry herself with elegance, how to wear the latest fashions straight from Paris, and which perfume to wear to match the activity she was attending. She encouraged Nena to imitate the Hollywood stars she had seen in the local movie house. Emulating Audrey Hepburn, Ava Gardner, and Joan Crawford, Nena learned how to wear her hair, how to hold her cigarette, how to make an entrance. *Etiquetta y protocolo* was taken to a new level. She met international celebrities and even had Zsa Zsa Gabor eat *Salcocho*, a traditional Dominican soup, in her house. She accepted many invitations to the home of Trujillo. Ramfi Trujillo, the son of the dictator, and Pirulo were very close, and Nena socialized with them often.

Pirulo was proud to have Nena on his arm. With the help of his mother to package the very young beauty, this Dominicana, he could show his countrymen the values of the European ways. He could show that Nena (and all the women who could "pass for white") was an example of the transformations the current government wanted for all of them.

Nena, in turn, was given all of the material possessions she could want. She knew how to play her role well and at first immersed herself in following the orders of her lover.

Nena began to realize she was a prisoner of this family, a nightmare first manifested when Pirulo's jealousy, at first flattering, became abusive. Pirulo so controlled Nena that he forbade her from looking sideways while riding in the car, accusing her of looking at other men. This control turned into violence. The first physical incident occurred when, seated next to him at a gambling table, she exchanged a few words with another man. Pirulo backhanded her so hard across the face that she fell to the ground. The violence escalated to regular beatings and torture. Pirulo's sadistic violence against his fellow Dominicans, especially those accused of conspiring against Trujillo, was part of his daily work activities. It seemed that when he came home to Nena, he could not turn this off.

An example occurred one day when he came home to find Nena sleeping on the floor of the living room, something she did because the marble kept her cool from the tropical heat. He found it offensive that his woman should display herself this way for the servants to see. He grabbed her by the hair, slammed the back of her head against the floor, dragged her across the room, and rammed her head again against the wall. Later that evening, she was expected to look her best for dinner with his colleagues. (Of her sexual humiliation—that is, repeated rape—and of Pirulo's specific assignments on behalf of Trujillo that he carried out, Nena refuses to talk about. She is still convinced someone out there is keeping tabs on her and will come after her family if she betrays El Generalisimo, who has been dead for decades. "*Eso quedo borrado* [That remains erased]," she tells me firmly.)

At the age of sixteen, Nena gave birth to her first child, Carmen Rosa. The child brought a brief respite from the beatings, as the couple's lives revolved around this joy. Nena adored her baby girl and showered her with affection. Carmen Rosa in turn became very attached to her mommy. The two were enveloped in bliss. Carmen Rosa was also the excuse for Nena to see her parents more often. Mama helped in taking care of the baby, and Leonte began to make regular visits.

Nena's father, Leonte, had by then begun to drink large amounts of alcohol daily, and his finances were dwindling. Leda (my mother's stepmother and his legitimate wife) left him, and the rest of his children were dispersed to their respective mothers. On one of Leonte's visits, he witnessed the abuse that Pirulo inflicted on his daughter, causing great pain and humiliation to Leonte. Despite his weakened state, he stood between Nena and her murderous husband as much as he could, making idle threats. Once, Pirulo wanted to show Leonte the degree to which he possessed Nena by pointing a gun at her. While Nena crouched down in terror, Pirulo laughed. Leonte stood between Nena and the gun, pleading for this madness to end—a madness that possessed the entire island. More sadness, however, was to come their way.

Pregnant with Pirulo's second child, Nena napped with Carmen Rosa, then two years old. She was awakened from this siesta by a slimy sensation crawling on her face. She looked over to Carmen Rosa and saw long worms crawling out of her baby girl's nostrils. Within days, Carmen Rosa died of an overwhelming parasitic infection.

Nena was so distraught she couldn't go to the funeral. For weeks, she spoke to no one. She was in a stupor, staring out into empty space. One of her few activities was caressing Carmen Rosa's dresses and hair ribbons while rocking on the chair where she had fed, kissed, cuddled, and sang to her baby. Leonte was sure his daughter would die of a broken heart, and others worried about the harm to the second child she was carrying. Mama had chills when she saw Nena withdrawn into her inner world.

The excruciating pain of labor brought Nena out of her catatonia. She seemed to come back to life when she begged for her mother. "*Mama, por favor, ayudame que te necesito*[Mama, help me, I need you]."

It was in this state of mind that Nena gave birth to Gilberto Sanchez Rodriguez on June 25, 1955.

Pirulo was ecstatic to have a son, his namesake. He beamed with pride, and for a short while afterward, he kept his violent hands off of Nena.

After coming out of her stupefaction and giving birth, Nena was not the same person. Anger and rage began to consume her. Nothing in this home, in this relationship, pleased her anymore. Leaving her comfortable surroundings to sleep in bed with Mama in her humble home was all she wanted. By the time Gilbert was a toddler, that was all he wanted as well. A son who rejected his father and a woman who began to hate the sight of him made Pirulo react violently toward them. Then one day, he just let them go. Nena and Gilbert moved in with Mama and Neida, Nena's sister. The freedom was granted because Pirulo then married a woman with "high" social standing and with her had another boy, also named Gilberto, and a girl who died liked his other baby girl.

His father provided for Gilbert, but Nena wanted to provide for Mama and to make her life comfortable. Nena was also growing tired of living on the island, becoming desperate to see the world, meet different people, and learn new ideas. She became a stewardess. The airline supervisors put her through a vigorous training of first-response emergency duties and educated her on the finer points of the service industry. Her job was to help the customers while remaining sexy.

Nena loved her job. Her routes were from the capital city, Santo Domingo, to Caracas, Venezuela, Port Au Prince, Haiti, and San Juan, Puerto Rico. She was always in a good mood when wearing her uniform and planning for the next trip. This job gave her the perfect outlet for someone feeling claustrophobic in her small country and allowed her the means to financially support Mama and Neida.

Nena left the airline industry after surviving a plane accident. Her thoughts then turned toward going abroad to live. Her friends who had left Dominican Republic were either in Paris or New York. "*En este infierno no me quedo yo* [I am not staying in this hell]." She began writing them letters and planned on visiting some of them.

Her anxiety and irritability, while out of work, made her develop a very itchy rash on her legs that turned into long, unsightly welts. She saw a doctor, who diagnosed a minor condition known as Lichen Planus. "*Si me lo quierro curar enseguida, a cual pais tendría que ir* [If I wanted this cured right away, which country should I go to]?" she asked as an idea hatched.

"*Estados Unidos,*" answered the doctor. At Nena's request, he wrote her a letter of medical necessity to travel abroad. She took the letter to Ramfi Trujillo, with whom she remained friendly.

Leaving the island was all but impossible during this time. Several months earlier, an attempt to overthrow Trujillo was made on June 14, 1959. A group of Dominicans living abroad as well as within the island, with the backing of Fidel Castro, attacked on this date. Trujillo's army quickly squashed this attempt. However, an opposition movement had been born, known as *Movimiento catorce de Junio.* With this brazen attack against the dictator, the international community became aware of the growing discontent within this island led by a dictator whom the United States supported.

Fearing that this movement would signal the beginning of the end for his regime, El Generalisimo Trujillo cracked down severely on anyone suspected of being a part of this conspiracy. Dominicans were watched closely, suspects were interrogated and tortured at several notorious sites, and many people "disappeared" during this period of terror. Life was oppressive, everyone watching each other with suspicious eyes and careful of whom to trust. It made Nena's desire to leave even more urgent, for she felt she could not live under this strangulation.

Ramfis Trujillo, the dictator's son, gave Nena a letter requesting she be allowed out of the country due to medical necessity. The day he gave her the letter, she received her three-month visa to the United States. Within a week of getting the visa, Nena was on her way to New York, landing in the big city on September 17, 1959.

(When I asked Nena, doubtfully, why Ramfis would do this for her, given the historical fact that anyone even requesting to leave the country at this time was considered a traitor to the Dictator, she simply answered, "Because he was my friend.")

Nena in New York City

"*Esto es una maravilla. Yo no se ni para donde mirar* [This is all a marvel. I don't even know where to look]," Nena said while staring up at the skyscrapers.

"*Cuidado, Nena, que aquí las gente andan tan rapido que te tumban y siguen como si nada* [Careful, Nena. People here are always in a rush. They'll knock you down and just keep walking like nothing happened]," said her friend Gladys, who was letting Nena stay with her.

Nena was in a state of exhilaration upon arriving in New York City, the city she had heard so much about from her father who had lived there, the city she had seen in movies and magazines, the city she had read about in newspapers, especially those articles profiling celebrities who lived here. She felt herself lifted out of reality and into a wonderful dream.

Nena was there in the flesh, absorbing and observing the energy and high activity level with order beneath the chaos. She loved the fact that the sidewalks were paved, the streets were numbered, addresses could be found with precision, and the trains and buses ran on a predictable schedule. Historical sites were right in front of her eyes. "*Ese es Central Park* [That's Central Park]?" She let out a yell.

"*Shh, tranquila, Nena. Aquí la gente no anda gritando como en el campo* [Shh, calm down, Nena. Here people don't go around screaming like in the back woods]," Gladys said. They broke into laughter, hugged, and continued walking down Fifth Avenue arm in arm.

Nena was sharing a dorm room with Gladys on 110th Street and Broadway in Manhattan. Gladys was a childhood friend from San Juan de la Maguana who had been sent to New York City to study. Thrilled to have this friend from back home, Gladys invited Nena to stay with her. Gladys took Nena to her doctor's appointment even though the rash on her legs was by now practically gone. Because Nena was, after all, given her travel visa due to medical necessity, she needed to have a doctor's visit documented. "*Bueno, Nena, ya que estas aquí, disfruta la visita* [Well, Nena, now that you're here, you might as well enjoy your visit]," Gladys said.

Nena could not contain herself and began treating herself to luxuries unavailable back home. She bought designer clothing, treated herself to facials at Elizabeth Arden Salon, and set about to discover a new restaurant every day.

Nena was falling in love with New York City. She felt she could be whomever she wanted. And even though her vanity still required careful attention to clothes and makeup, she was beginning to calm down on this self-imposed pressure, no longer needing to worry that she had to look her best all the time as the mother of Pirulo's child. She had left an island that had so many problems and a dictator obsessed with his public's personal hygiene and style. In New York, no one cared what she looked like or who she was—the city where the prince and pauper walked side by side.

She was also free from the fear that the secret police could show up at her house at any time to get a full accounting of her days. If they didn't like the answers they got or were suspicious of her friends being subversives, they could make her sweat out an unpleasant interrogation.

Here she dated men from different backgrounds who took her to new restaurants, different neighborhoods, museums, and live shows. These men were mostly Gringos with whom, in her heart, she knew she couldn't connect. "*Son tan son-so* [They're so bland]," she told Gladys. She kept on dating them, however, because it was fun and because she was running out of money. She simply could not afford this extended vacation much longer.

The other realization that was beginning to take hold of her was that she didn't want to go back home.

As she thought about this fact, she stepped into the elevator on her way out for more sightseeing. She was greeted by the most beautiful man she had ever seen in her life. He lifted his hat off of his greased back hair and said to her, "*Encantado, soy Angel Maseda.*" Nena became breathless, nervous, and excited. Her blood rushed to her head, and the adrenaline made her heart thump. It was love at first sight with this Cubano.

Angel Maseda became the only man Nena truly loved.

(For the rest of her life, Nena would retell the story of her arrival to New York City with the emphasis that those were the happiest days of her life.)

I Want to Live in America

Nena and Angel on their wedding day

(From jfklibrary.org: "In 1960, President Eisenhower approved a plan by the Central Intelligence Agency to train Cuban exiles for an invasion of their homeland. The ultimate goal was the overthrow of Castro and the establishment of a noncommunist government friendly to the United States. Shortly after his inauguration in February 1961, President Kennedy authorized the invasion plan."

Nena is in the kitchen chopping onions that will be added to the *Fabada* Angel Maseda is making for his guests. A group of his Cuban friends have come over for another meeting to plan their roles as participants in an invasion of Cuba—a confrontation that Cubans living abroad hope will win back their island from Fidel Castro's regime. Juan Pan Piro, always dressed in white and chain smoking cigars, exclaims, "*Cuando agarre a ese barbudo hijo de la gran puta, lo voy a descualtilizar* [When I grab that bearded son of a bitch, I am going to dismember him]."

"*Fidel Castro, ya no duro mucho; nosotros lo vamos acabar* [Fidel Castro won't last long; we're going to finish him off]," says Angel.

As Nena listens to Angel and his friends describe how he is going to decapitate Fidel, chop his balls off, pull out his finger nails one by one, etc., she feels the anger rising within her. For weeks, this is all she's heard.

After meeting Angel in the elevator in the spring of 1960, Nena's life was devoted to being by the side of this handsome, charismatic Cubano who was full of dreams about how he was going to "make it" in the Big Apple Latin music scene. Angel reunited with some of his musician friends who had also left Cuba, such as Miguelito Valdes with whom he was planning to open up a Latin club where people could enjoy dancing *el mambo*. Angel had been a promoter and heavily involved with the nightclub scene in Havana. With the exodus of more artists to the United States, Angel wanted to position himself such that he would help launch careers for Cuban musicians in New York City. His nightclub would offer a venue for them.

Nena loved going out with Angel to the Palladium Ballroom, El Club Caborroejeno on 145th and Broadway, and the St. Nicholas Ballroom. These were places where they spent many happy hours dancing. For more authentic *son*, they would go to the South Bronx where Arsenio Rodriguez lived and spend time at Club Cubano Inter-Americano, where Cubans and Puerto Ricans came together to socialize, listen to live music, and dance. Through these connections, Angel and Tito Rodriguez (who was born in Puerto Rico to a Dominican father and a Cuban mother) became close friends, and it helped Angel move forward with these business plans.

Angel repeatedly told Nena how much he loved New York—the energy, the music, meeting people from all over the world. He had many Puerto Rican musician friends and embraced an awakening that he was part of the larger Latino community. Nena and Angel had fallen in love with each other and with their new lives. Together, they did what so many immigrants have always done—reinvent themselves.

During the rounds of Christmas season partying in 1960, Nena became pregnant. She had by then overstayed her visa because parting with Angel was impossible for her. Angel took her to city hall in early 1961, making her wish come true, to be married to him. There was never anything Nena wanted more than this. This period in her life was blissful.

"So now what's he doing out there talking about fighting in some invasion? What about me? This life in New York that they have created for themselves, what will happen if the invasion is successful and Angel feels he needs to return to Cuba? Besides, what are they all talking about? Why didn't they fight when they had the chance instead of running away from their Cuba they claim to love so much?" Nena is angrily obsessing. Hearing them trying to be big men is making her internal temperature rise. She's becoming lightheaded with anger, her blood is boiling, and the anger is about to spill over. She stabs the wooden cutting board with the big chopping knife.

"*En esta sala no hay hombres*[I don't see any men this living room]!" she blasts. Angel Maseda looks at her startled; his eyes warn her to stop. Juan Pan Piro's cigar falls out of his mouth, and some of the other men chuckle, thinking this is a joke.

"*Porque el hombre, que es hombre de verdad, se quedo en Cuba* [The real Cuban man remained in Cuba]," she continues. "*Ustedes nadamas sirven para hablar, pero alla no hablan así. Todo lo que estan diciendo aquí, vayan y dícelo a Fidel, a que no se atreven. Coño, para sacar a los Españoles de Cuba tuvo Maximo Gomez, un Dominicano, que ir y liberalos. Pero ahora, no esperen que los Dominicanos vengan a sarval la balsa de cobardes.* [You only talk that way here. Why don't you tell Fidel Castro these things to his face? Maximo Gomez, a Dominican, had to liberate Cuba from Spanish rule. But don't wait for a Dominican to save you bunch of cowards now]." Nena is on a roll castrating these men.

No one can stop her, despite Angel's attempts. The men leave while Nena's voice becomes louder. They give their condolences to Angel for what to them seems like an unbearable woman. "*Sí largensen porque la verdad no la quierren oír* [Yes, leave, you don't want to hear the truth]," Nena puts her last words in.

After the last of the men leave, Angel gets in Nena's face and starts yelling at her. "*Eres una loca! Como te atreves hablarme de esa manera en frente de mis amigos* [You're crazy! How dare you embarrass me in front of my friends]." He grabs her by the shoulders, starts shaking her, and when she opens her mouth to speak, he slaps her across the face.

"*You jure, coño, que el ultimo hombre que a mí me pondría una mano violenta fue Gilberto Sanchez Rubirosa* [I swore that Gilberto Sanchez Rubirosa would be the last man who would ever lay a violent hand on me]." As she says these words, she grabs a bottle of olive oil and throws it at Angel, hitting him square on the forehead. Startled by what she just did, Nena runs out of the apartment.

Hours after the incident, Angel finds Nena crying in a neighbor's kitchen. She gives him an angry look although inside, when she sees him with the flowers, she feels ecstasy. The relationship is not over after all. She was sure that after this outburst, she could not repair the damage. She doesn't know why this happens to her—the anger, the rage that turns into a blinding fury, and before she realizes it, she is acting violently. For the moment, what matters is that he's here, and he forgives her.

"*Mi amor, perdoname. Tu sabes que te quierro mas que a mi mismo. Pero tienes que entender como se juega el juejo* [My love, I love you more than my own life, but you have to understand how to play the game]." He softly caresses her hair, and she buries her face in his chest and begs him not to go and fight. "*Yo no tengo la menor intencion de ir a peliar, peliar para que? Si aqui lo tengo todo. Pero hay que hablar de cierta manera para que los Yanquis se crean que los hemos perdido todo* [I have no intention of going to fight. Fight for what? Everything I need is right here. But you have to talk a certain way so the Yankees think we Cubans have lost it all to Fidel]." Nena starts laughing uncontrollably. What she loves the most about Angel is his storytelling. He can convince a crowd of almost anything, and if she's in on the delusional content, there just isn't anything more entertaining than to watch him in action. She has never met, heard of, or experienced anything like this charismatic Angel Maseda and how he can enrapture a crowd with fabricated tales.

"*Angel, tu si eres un cuento* [Angel, you are a piece of fiction]," she tells him in between her laughter. He swoops her in his arms as the neighbors watch this master of the golden tongue work his magic.

That night, taking advantage of the position Nena put herself in by scaring away his Cuban friends, Angel has Nena call the leader of the group to let him know that Angel Maseda will not be partaking of the Bay of Pigs Invasion because of her pregnancy. The friends all understand. Angel saves face, stays in New York, and the business of getting a Latino nightclub opened up is back in planning.

With the Bay of Pigs situation behind him, Angel's thoughts turn to renting the Audoban Ballroom on Broadway and putting together a night of salsa dancing featuring Perez Prado. An evolution in music is occurring with the rhythm of *son* in New York City giving birth to salsa. Finding venues where people can dance to these new sounds is Angel's business at this time. People can't get enough of the mambo. In addition, Angel will promote these musicians until the nightclub he is obsessed with finally opens.

As he holds his Dominican fireball and does the two-step to the Congo sounds of Mongo Santamaria, they laugh at the Gringos who will soon start complaining about the loud music.

Nena's Dilemma

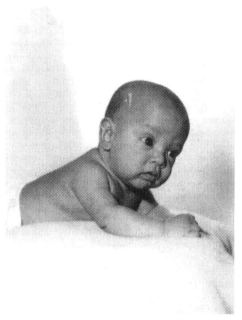

Pepin several months old

Nena looks at herself in the mirror, rubs her lips together after applying her favorite lipstick, tangy, and strikes a pose. "I'm much too skinny," she tells the woman in the mirror, but no time for obsessing over her flat butt. She's going to party tonight!

It's been a long time since she and Angel had a night out with their friends. Today is New Year's Eve, 1961, and she's been stuck in the apartment since bringing home her premature baby in September. He was born August 1, 1961, after Nena went into spontaneous labor weeks before his due date. He spent one month in the intensive care unit where his life was an uncertainty at first.

After the first week of the baby's life, the doctors told Angel and Nena their son would make it if he put on the necessary weight. Every day, Nena walked to the hospital, stood next to her son's incubator, and helplessly looked at him. Nena saw her little boy struggle to breathe, suffer through tube feedings, and occasionally cry. She had no energy, no strength, and wanted to sleep all of the time.

(When Nena would retell this story over the following decades, she admits she really did not know what she felt during this time, probably numbness, especially when she would hear that another of this cohort of newborns, had died.)

On the baby's tenth day of life, Nena saw her son flare his arms up. She was startled and excited to see that he seemed stronger and even had signs of an emerging personality. Nena knew then he was going to survive. Jose Antonio Maseda was going to live.

She fell in love with this little creation when that arm went up and moved beyond the swaddle of the blanket. She wanted this baby home with her more than anything. To her, it was as if his defying death in this neonatal intensive care unit was his way of loving her. When he was strong enough to be held, Nena looked into those big eyes and wondered how she could ever have been ambivalent about wanting him. She now began preparing for his homecoming, cleaning up the extra bedroom and filling it with discarded pieces of furniture her husband, the superintendent of the building, had first dibs on. While previously she dreaded the idea of dragging herself to the hospital to see that little body struggling for life, now she couldn't wait to get to the hospital and hold her bundle. She even began chatting with the nurses in her broken English and had nicknames for the other preemies. "That one is a raisin, and that one a plucked chicken, and this one here, well, no one knows what he's capable of." The day she was told Pepin could go home in forty-eight hours, she whisked the swaddled bundle into her arms and started dancing merengue with him pressed against her chest, while the nurses clapped to Nena's humming. A dramatic change was observed by the hospital staff. That zombie-like person who would just stare at the incubator and not interact with the staff was now a woman full of energy, optimism, laughter, and abundant affection for her boy.

The honeymoon between Nena and Jose did not last long after bringing him home. The worry about a vulnerable child began turning into a confused anger. The careful around-the-clock feeds, the constant cleaning up of his vomit, the correct positioning of the weak body—nothing seemed to appease his almost constant crying and irritability. The days were getting shorter and colder, so she dared not take him outside. Angel became more involved with his music business, and she would see him for only about an hour a day before he fell asleep. She was spinning into madness. The rage was consuming. The churning feeling inside could not be contained, and violence followed. She found herself sometimes smacking Jose across his bald head or screaming at him with their noses touching, cursing, "*Porque tuve que parir* [Why did I have this child]?" The guilt afterward made her sick, in pain and despair, and she felt like she was slipping into a very cold, deep, dark hole. She couldn't eat; after bringing him home, she was practically living on cigarettes and "café Bustelo."

She tells the lady in the mirror, "*A bailar se ha dicho* [We're going to dance tonight]." Nena and Angel ring in the New Year dancing, laughing, eating all their favorite foods, and getting drunk. Back home, intoxicated on the joys of this night, they fall into a ravenous session of love making.

"*Hay coño,*" she says, laughing as she runs to the bathroom to douche herself after Angel ejaculated. "I didn't put my diaphragm on!" They're both finding this contraceptive attempt hilarious and are laughing hysterically as Nena rinses out her vaginal vault as thoroughly as possible.

By the middle of February 1962, Nena has not left the apartment in days. Jose's crying wakes her up, but the nausea and retching prevents her from responding to her baby, who is only now starting to sleep four to five hours at night. She lies in bed wishing there were someone she could call for help, but all of her family is in the Dominican Republic. She's made some friends in New York City, but certainly no one close enough to ask if they can come over and help her with her baby. Besides, here everyone is always busy with work, their own chores, their own children. Nena cannot wait for the day she can go back to work, doing anything that'll get her out of the house. Even that factory job where she sewed the exact pattern of dresses over and over again all day was better than this. However, right now, making it to the crib is taking up every ounce of strength and energy she can recruit.

She heats a bottle of milk, and as she feeds Pepin, her son's nickname, she knows she's pregnant again. The despair has her almost paralyzed, and she spends hours just staring blankly into space and praying for just a little bit more energy to deal with her boy. Only one thought gives her hope, gives her that one string to hang onto, to keep her going—that soon this pregnancy will be terminated.

A few days later, she's feeling better as she sits with Angel watching television, snacking on cold chicken with their pajamas on. Nena gets up to go to the kitchen in her see-through nylon nightdress. Angel says, "*No te lo saques* [Don't terminate the pregnancy]. This one is going to be a girl, and we both know how much you want a little girl." Nena comes over, sits on his lap, and he starts rocking her. She is so weak in this state. He's kissing her, running his hand through her hair, and describing the pleasures of a baby girl. "A girl will be your best friend for life," he says. He gives her the visual image of the dresses trimmed in lace, doing her hair with ribbons, piercing her ears.

For Nena, it's a chance to reclaim a girl after losing her two-year-old daughter in the Dominican Republic. But no! After what she's gone through these past months with a needy, sick, premature baby, the rage at not being able to go out for days due to the cold weather, the four walls closing in on her—no, no, no. "I just can't do it again . . . and if it's a boy, I'll just . . ."

Angel tells her to stand up and walk across the living room. He says he can predict whether it's a boy or a girl by the way Nena moves.

"Yep, it's a girl all right."

Elated, she crawls back onto his lap where he begins the story of this new addition to the family, this little girl who will bring joy to the home and complete the family.

On September 16, 1962, Nelly Maria Dolores Maseda was born.

The Bigamist

Tito Rodriguez(left) shaking hands with Perez-Prado(right)
Angel Maseda next to Perez-Prado (your right)
Raul Quintana (co-owner of **El Bronx Casino** and Nelly's godfather)
inbetween Tito Rodriguez and Perez-Prado in front of **El Bronx Casino**
Date Unknown
Found by Nelly Maseda on a **Google** search of **El Bronx Casino** in early
2001.

Nena is sitting on the arm of our living room couch, staring at the television, tapping her foot, and smoking one cigarette after another. It is 1966 in New York City. Nena is waiting for the few hours of Spanish television that come on at night. She's gotten out of her pajamas, which she's been wearing for days, and her bony figure now has on a tight, black skirt.

Pepin and I are playing on the splintered wooden living room floor with a Silly Putty. Pepin, a creative artist, contorts the putty into different shapes, and the game is for me to guess what the new sculpture represents. "What's this?" he asks

"A *platano*," I respond. We both blurt out with laughter. We hug and roll over each other, and I yell out, "Eeeeee!" as we're so excited.

He smiles at me and says, "Tomorrow, Pops is going to come in through that door with so many presents they're going to touch the ceiling." We hug each other with so much joyful anticipation that we roll along the floor. The two little bodies of a four—and a five-year-old are inseparable in their magical world of sibling oneness.

"Shut up!" my mother screams. Pepin and I sit up at attention, and my older half-brother, Gilbert, sprints into the living room when he hears her shriek. Gilbert, now eleven years old, spends most of his time hanging out on the rooftop of this building or in the park on 173rd Street. Today he's gotten a beating from my mother as she yelled, "You keep your black ass home tonight for Christmas, *negro del diablo*." He's always in trouble and has already spent more days of this school year suspended from school than in attendance.

Earlier today, Nena was so angry when she found Gilbert smoking pot on the roof that she gave him a beating sure to keep him behaving well for a few days. She dragged him into the apartment by the straps of his overalls, yelling, "*Maldito Negro, porque te traje ha este país* [Negro, why did I bring you to this country]?" She proceeded toward the bathroom where she held him down with his face directly underneath the stream of water. She let the bathtub fill, submerging him, while she alternated the hot and cold water, making sure the water hit Gilbert directly on the face. Pepin and I hugged each other as we heard the splashing of water, Gilbert gasping for air when he momentarily fought his way out of each near drowning round, and Nena yelling, "I'm gonna kill you!"

As a result of the tumultuous events occurring in the Dominican Republic after the country's dictator was killed in 1961, Gilbert's father wanted his son to leave the country. However, none of Trujillo's men or their families were allowed to leave the country, as many of them were going to face justice for their crimes. One of those to be persecuted was Pirulo. He appealed to my mother for help in bringing their child to New York City. Nena called her father, Leonte, for help. Leonte paid to have a false birth certificate issued on behalf of my brother, changing his name from Gilberto Sanchez Rodriguez to Gilberto Rodriguez, and listed as his parents on this new document were Nelia Rodriguez as the mother and Leonte Rodriguez as the father. In a poor country, such as this one, new "official" documents were easy to purchase, and people were thereby able to reinvent themselves for a small price.

On the New York City end of this plot, Angel Maseda cooperated with all of the necessary paperwork for his stepson to join us (as he did for the eventual immigration of Nena's siblings). Angel embraced his stepson and was openly affectionate toward him. Gilbert became so attached to Angel that the absences took their toll on the stepchild as well. With Angel spending less time in our home, Gilbert found solace in the streets.

When my father visits after his long absences, we all act as if he'd never left. He sleeps in bed with my mother, and the morning after, always in a good mood, he cooks breakfast. "My *lindos*, do you want eggs ranchero style today?" We come running to him, the three of us attacking his soft body while he sings, "Baseball, hot dog, apple pie, and Chevrolet." He releases us to take a sip of whiskey. Tonight, Angel is not here.

My mother jumps forward toward the black and white television set and raises the volume. As she goes back to the spot at the edge of the couch, she stares at us, and with a pointed finger, cigarette burning, she yells, "I don't want to hear a word out of your mouths!" and menaces us with the leather belt.

What we see on television, however, overwhelms us. Pepin and I start jumping up and down, screaming, "Papi! Papi!" We hold each other's hands and start spinning around the room.

Gilbert's eyes widen as he exclaims, "Holy shit, Angel is on television! My man is on *el show de Pumarejo*." *Pumarejo* was at the time to the Latino community what the *Johnny Carson Show* was to the mainstream population. And tonight, the featured guest is my father, Angel Maseda.

"I saaaiid, not one peep out of your mouths!" my mother yells as she folds over the leather belt. Holding each end, she makes a loop and then a quick snapping sound as she quickly closes the loop. This silences us. The belt comes out more often when Angel is not around and her mood darkens. If she isn't sleeping, she's yelling at us to be quiet, to move out of her way, and wondering out loud why she ever had us.

My handsome Cuban father with his movie star good looks is on television being interviewed about his night club, El Bronx Casino. It's a salsa club where many *soneros* perform live. My father is smiling, speaking animatedly about his latest talent-scout find. His hair is greased back, and he is elegantly holding a cigarette in one hand. He is wearing a tuxedo to mark this festive occasion where his club is hosting an all-night dance party with live music. I focus in on the slight gap between his teeth and feel my face against his chest. I can even smell the cigarette smoke on him. I miss him. I'm scared. I don't know what my mother is capable of doing to us tonight.

Nena leans forward toward the television, taking in every single word he says. Her irritability is palpable as she crushes one cigarette, lights another, and puts her free hand back on the leather belt besides her. We are all aware now as the interview progresses with, not a mention of us, that in this Christmas season we are not on his mind. In fact, as he becomes more involved in his other affairs, he forgets my family.

One of these other affairs was my father's recent trip to Florida to pick up his other family who had just arrived from Cuba. He set up that wife and three children in a house in Queens. We were in Manhattan, and with his girlfriend, a Puerto Rican singer by the name of Miriam Alonso, he shared an apartment in the Bronx.

(Forgetting about my family meant taking away his larger than life celebrity personality. His warmth, his jokes, his storytelling lifted my mother to such heights of happiness, she didn't care if he had one hundred other girlfriends, as long as he came home to her. That's all we needed. His absence condemned us to the suffering of missing his irreplaceable self, leaving us to the danger of a mother with the unpredictability of what her severe mood swings would expose us to. It left us in poverty, as she was rarely able to hold a job, and it left us to walk that tightrope of our lives, trying to keep the peace with my mother.)

"Look at him," she says as the interview on television is now ending, "and not even a whistle this Christmas for his children." She goes over to the two-foot-tall Christmas tree and kicks it over. She stands back in front of the television, cigarette in one hand, and points at the screen with a free finger. "You told me you loved me, you bastard. I married you, and then you threw these kids at me like saying 'deal with it,' and there you are laughing—typical Cuban bullshitter. You all come running to this country talking about Fidel. Well, what have you cowards done to get your country back? Nothing! All you do is talk, talk, talk. You talked me into these kids with your golden tongue—and for what? I curse each day I gave birth to them . . ." Her voice becomes louder and more desperate during the fight with the image before her. We tiptoe into the bedroom, hoping she won't smash up the television set. We hold on to each other in bed, eager for this rant to soon be over.

Christmas 1967

It was a cold December morning, and we therefore had to play indoors. We were racing our toy cars on the unpolished, splintered wooden floor. The excitement of the Christmas spirit was upon us, and we began to talk about our wish lists. "I want the dancing ballerina, the one you pull the crown to make her dance," I said at five years old.

"I want the super deluxe Mattel racing track, the one with long curves and the gasoline filling station," Pepin said, swaying his open arms, gesticulating as he said the word "curves." He was six years old.

Ochie, my three-year-old cousin, Neida's son, said with the sweetest smile, "I want *un cheeseburger sin queso* [a cheeseburger without cheese]."

Pepin and I laughed so hard we just had to hug and kiss Ochie for his cuteness. We were always so affectionate with each other. Hugging, kissing, and squeezing each other tight with no inhibitions and no reason needed to just press our faces together, cheek to cheek.

Upon hearing our wish lists, my mother, who was already in one of her irritable moods and who had already yelled at us to "keep it down," came over to us. "*Chrima, Chrima, coño, yo te voy a decir que coño es Chrima* [I'm going to tell you the fucking truth about Christmas]." She proceeded to grab us individually by our shirts and lift us up onto her bedroom dresser with the mirror behind us. After the three of us were seated, she paced back and forth and began her speech.

She looked at us, her face flushed with anger, her eyes squinting, and her voice the shrill of a woman on the verge. We listened very quietly, nervous and wondering what punishment was coming our way for doing who knows what. "This woman you see standing right before you is your mother, your father, the Easter bunny, and Santa Claus." (My concrete mind was visualizing this ninety-pound woman in a Santa outfit). "*Chrima* was invented by Jews to make poor people like us empty our wallets buying junk to make them even richer. Whitey up there is laughing at us, at how stupid we are and how easy it is to fill our heads, thinking we need all their piece of crap toys that break right away. There are people out there shooting each other on the streets so their children could have something under the tree to open up on Christmas day." She brings her face close up against ours and continues, "Buy this, buy that, I want this, I want that god-damnit, all to make us crazy . . . Where the hell do you think those toys are going to come from? Shit, if there really were some **comemierda** up there handing out free things, you think we'd be in this rat hole? I'm the one that has to go out there and try to find the money to buy you these toys, and with what? *Porque pesos no tengo, pero pelos sí tengo bastante* [Dollars I don't have, but hairs I've got plenty]," she stated, pointing to her pubic area.

After this great uninterrupted speech, she lit up a cigarette and went back to the kitchen table to *calcular los numeritos*, calculate which would be the winning number of the day.

Pepin helped us down from the bureau, put one arm around Ochie's shoulder and the other around mine, and walked us back to our game with the toy cars. He said, "Guys, it's true what she said. There is no Santa Claus, but on Christmas Day, Pops is going to walk in through that door with so many toys the boxes will reach the ceiling. And when Mom sees him, she'll be so happy that they're going to start kissing. We're going to have the best Christmas ever."

"Aaayy!" I yelled. "I just got another splinter in my foot."

"Shh," said Pepin. "I'll take it out. Just keep your voice down so Mom won't hear us."

Santo Domingo—The Divorce

I remember when my parents divorced, Nena cried silently as she packed all the items up from our apartment on 169th Street and Ft. Washington Avenue. She decided we were going to live in the Dominican Republic. Before we left to the airport, my father met us in the lobby of our building, dressed in a suit, sitting on a bench. My mother gave me a book and told me to give it to him. It was a large, heavy, hard cover, and I walked over to him trembling because, although I wasn't fully aware of the specifics, I knew something terrible was happening. He was not joining us on this trip. He smiled at me, the echoing of the heels of my white, patent leather shoes marking time in what seemed like an endless march.

I remember walking into the jumbo jet, Pepin ahead of me. Pepin and I looked at the row of seats, turned to face each other, and lunged, locking our heads into a wrestling position. Instinctively, we knew we needed to fight over the window seat. He won.

I remember arriving in the heat of the tropics, wearing a party dress and making sure my Easter hat stayed on my head. In Tamara's house, my mother's sister, the first thing my aunt noticed was how I held a fork with my thumb on the rear of the utensil. She taught me how to properly hold a fork. "*Etiqueta y protocolo,*" she told me as she hugged and kissed me.

I remember a neighborhood fair where Pepin won a bicycle race and was rewarded with a ribbon pinned over his upper left chest. His little blond head going up and down while he was cycling on a bike Angel bought us. He taught himself to ride a two-wheeler and during this trip taught me. I remember repeatedly falling off the bike. Pepin would pick me up, dust me off, hold onto the bicycle seat, and try again until I learned.

I remember once Nena and Tamara rearranging furniture in the living room, Tamara singing "Senor City Lights" to the tune of a Frank Sinatra song. "No, Tamara, *es* 'Strangers in the Night,'" Nena corrected her, laughing. Tamara's face turned serious as she comforted Nena, who was now crying while saying, "*Es que esa cancion me recuerda de Angel* [It's just that this song reminds me of Angel]."

I remember during this trip a large flying cockroach landing on my face while I slept. I woke up with a startle. Nena, Pepin, and several other women were in the room sleeping with us. They all started laughing. Pepin hugged and kissed the cheek where the cockroach had landed. "Let's get the flying killer roaches. This place is crazy. What next? Talking *platanos*?" He and I were speaking English in the midst of heat, humidity, mutant insects, and random street bicycle races, just steps away from the starving children.

I remember the first time I saw scantily dressed children begging on the street, their empty eyes too hungry to show expression. I felt like I'd been punched in the stomach. I was only five years old when I first saw this vision of complete inhumanity. I couldn't stop crying but couldn't completely articulate what my inner pain was due to. All I could think about were the eyes of these starving children begging for food while others just went about their business. I remember a hamburger place we would go to late at night (was it called Chimichurri?). I remember the starving children would come running for the leftovers, and the restaurant patrons as well as the owner would shoo them away. The starving children were free game for anyone with power to kick and beat them as they pleased. (There hasn't been a single day of my life that I don't carry those children and their pain within me!)

I remember riding in the front of a car. My mother sat me on the lap of a male family friend. The car was packed, and in those days, the front seat did not have a divider. I remember this man put his hands over my vagina and massaged it during this car trip. I remember being very afraid and not knowing how I knew not to say anything. As this crime against a child occurred, everyone else in the car continued with their conversation, my vocal chords paralyzed.

I remember not seeing Gilbert very much. Where was he? Why wasn't he staying with us at Tamara's?

I remember having a febrile seizure. Actually, I remember coming out of the seizure biting my tongue. A doctor had come over and placed me in my cousins' infant bathtub that was filled with ice. As I awoke, Nena, the doctor, and Tamara each took turns dipping a towel into the ice, wrapping me with it, and carrying me around the room, gently soothing me.

When the scare was over, I remember Nena, Tamara, and the doctor went to the living room, and while they were out there talking and drinking coffee, Pepin came and lay down next to me. He patted my cheeks gently, and in our comforting English, he said "Nells, you okay?" His big, beautiful, hazel eyes in fright, he said, "You want some water, soup? Nell, I was so scared . . ."

We heard the voices from the living room conversing and Nena's volume rising. The Dominican Republic had been invaded by the United States. American symbols were all around, but the one that left its imprint on us were the large garbage bins on the street with the words "Safety Can" written on them. The Dominicans would pronounce it "Safacon," and it made an impression on us because after hearing this Spanglish translation, Nena giggled. It was one of the few times we heard my mother laugh during this trip. Now she was yelling at this very cultured doctor who had studied medicine in France, telling him, "*Ojala la Republica se convierta en otro Puerto Rico* [I wish Dominican Republic would have the same status as Puerto Rico]." Nena was obviously challenging the natives' desire for self-governance. She went on about how there hasn't been a single Dominican politician, a single Dominican male she's met that can be trusted. "Why would I want any of these men in power?" she questioned the doctor.

"There she goes, Godzilla versus King Kong," Pepin whispered in my ear. I tried to laugh but felt the fever rising, and as I looked around the room, distorted perceptions were taking hold with the bureau becoming gigantic and the door miniscule. The fever was rising, and I felt certain I would die that night.

The next morning, the brightness of the sun through the window awakened me. Nena was collecting and folding our clothing. "*Morena, mi muneca* [my doll]." She held and kissed me, softly running her fingers through my hair. Softly singing a Spanish song, she lay down between Pepin and me and continued to kiss and hug us both. "*Ustedes son mi alma* [You are my soul]," she told us as she showered affection on us and continued with her song. She told us we were leaving and going back to New York where we belonged.

She had considered staying in the Dominican Republic to live and work for a Venezuelan airline. She changed her mind because she felt I was constantly getting sick, that the tropical climate was too hard on me. She also realized that after having lived in New York, going back to her island to live was impossible for her.

Cup of Coins

Pepin and Nelita in Riverside Park 1960's

Nena wakes us up with her yelling, "*Coño, muchacho del Diablo, me-an-dote en la cama otra vez . . .*" Nonstop she rants about Pepin urinating on the bed the three of us have been sleeping together on since returning to New York City.

With the help of Angel Maseda, Nena was able to facilitate entry to the United States for six of her seven siblings, her biological mother, Ana Santana, and her stepmother, Leda Alcantara. (They in turn begin bringing to Washington Heights wives, in-laws, cousins, and so on.) Returning to New York, it is now Leda's turn to offer us a place to stay until Nena finds us our own apartment.

Pepin, Nena, and I share one bed next to Leda's sewing machine. Leda is a seamstress, and our bed is surrounded by made-to-order outfits hanging from a rope that runs the length of this rectangular room. Seven other people are living in this two-bedroom apartment on Audobon Avenue. Most of us are waiting to find our own place.

"Hurry up, Nelita," Nena says as she ties a silk scarf around her head babushka style. We are taking Leda's mother to Columbia Presbyterian Hospital today for a doctor's visit. I put on my blue wool coat, arrange my barrette carefully on my head, and pull my brown leather purse diagonally across my chest (I do not go anywhere without this purse). I'm staring at myself in the mirror, feeling like an adult because my mother kept me home from school so I can translate at the hospital.

Nena has Leda's mother's arm hooked into hers, and with her other hand, she holds mine. Nena carefully assists Leda's elderly mother down the staircase, through two sets of glass doors framed with metal, from the lobby toward the street. Slowly we cross the street headed for Broadway when I suddenly remember I left my cup of coins in the apartment.

On our flight back from the Dominican Republic, I kept a small, empty cup where coffee creamer had been distributed to the passengers. I placed a quarter inside and noticed how perfectly it fit within this container and proceeded to fill it up with loose change I had in my purse. The lid snapped tightly over the cup, and this became my wallet.

"Mommy, I forgot my money," I said.

"Okay, we'll wait for you here. Run up and get it. Papo is in the apartment, but hurry up, it's cold," she says while I carefully cross the street. I look back while entering the building to make sure she's looking at me. As I start to walk up the stairs, I see a group of black children, all around the same age as me, walking into the building. When I start knocking on our apartment door, the children surround me.

"Let's take the white girl to the roof," one of them says. I freeze, but I know that my uncle Papo will come to the door at any moment. They push me toward one another, and one of them punches my mouth. I instantly taste the saltiness of blood. Another grabs my purse strap, and they start pulling me toward the staircase. A boy grabs my arm and says, "I said, let's take her to the roof."

At this point, gripped in fear and starting to feel physical pain, I start yelling, "Mommy, Mommy, Mommy!" and I don't understand why Papo has not come out of the apartment with the noise we're making. In a panic, one of the children punches my mouth again and tells me to shut up. They trip me and drag me down the stairs. As my chin hits each step, I feel more blood coming out of my mouth but still manage to continue screaming, "Mommy, Mommy!"

When we reach the foot of the staircase, I look toward the double glass doors, and Nena is there blocking the child perpetrators as they try to escape. In her broken English, she is cursing these children out while slapping, kicking, and scratching each one. She has one kid on the floor with her foot on his chest and has grabbed one of the girls by the hair while taking swings at the others who are trying to get by her. Nena is in a fury. I hear one of them yell "Spic," and she yells back, "I am Dominican, *coño*. Don't you dare mess with us!"

Lying still, head on the floor, legs slanted upward on the stairs, and blood dripping from my mouth, I watch the rumble. I don't move. When the group finally breaks free of Nena's attack, she comes to me breathing heavily. Before picking me up, she holds my face in her hands, and I see the pain in her eyes as she struggles not to cry. She carries me upstairs, and with my head on her shoulders, she's banging on the apartment door while cursing Papo out in Spanish. With no response from him, she uses her own key to let us in.

We go straight to the bathroom sink where she starts washing my face. I look into the mirror and see the blood making outlines around my teeth. Nena tells me to keep rinsing out my mouth, and she stomps over to Papo who is fast asleep. "You lazy bum! Nelita almost got killed, and where were you?" He quickly comes over to me, and when he sees my beat-up face, tears swell in his eyes. He keeps hugging me while Nena continues to curse him out in Spanish.

"Well hurry up and get what you came for. We need to get to the hospital," she interrupts her rant against Papo. I run and get my cup, open the lid to make sure my money is still in there, and put it in my purse, which is still in its diagonal position. I'm shaking from my assault but relieved we are going to the hospital where I assume I'll be tended to.

On the corner of 171st Street and Broadway, I see a gumball machine and say, "Mommy, wait, I want to use my money to buy gum." I feel so grown up reaching into my purse, taking out my little plastic cup, unclasping the snug lid, removing a nickel, and getting my own gumball.

A few months later, in the summer of 1968, we are finally moving into our own apartment. It's a one-bedroom, fourth-floor walkup on 624 W. 176th Street. Mama, Neida, and Ochie are in a rented room a few blocks away. Leonte Rodriguez's children (with the exception of Tamara) are all settled in Washington Heights.

Although Nena and her siblings are all living within a few blocks of one another, I remember not wanting to leave Leda. She taught me how to sew and allowed me to practice by making clothes for my Barbie Doll using scraps of fabric. I loved it when she would allow me, with her hand over mine, to cut the fabric that had the paper patterns pinned to them for the clothes customers had ordered from her. I would miss watching *Lucha Libre* with her, sitting by as she and Pepin argued about whether or not the violence was real or staged, Leda insisting it was authentic fighting, despite Pepin acting out in detail for her how the moves were staged. I would miss watching her get up involuntarily from the rocking chair, fist in the air, when the masked enemy appeared on the screen to challenge one of her favorites, Bruno Sanmartino. I would miss how she misinterpreted English. For example, when the announcement on television was made, "We will be right back after station identification," and she heard, "I am taking a vacation," which made Pepin and I crack up. I planned to return as often as I could.

It only takes a few trips back and forth from Leda's apartment to refill our Alexander's Department Store large shopping bags, until we have all of our belongings moved. Two twin beds are already set up, and when the three of us look at them, Nena says, "You're going to sleep in your own bed. Finally, we're not going to wake up with your urine on us." His mattress has a plastic cover over it.

Someone knocks on the door while Nena is washing dishes on our first night there. An obese woman who lives next door greets us. "*Vengan a mi casa a tomar café,*" Rosalina invites us. She has a teenage daughter who takes out the game Parcheesi and starts playing with Pepin and me while Nena and Rosalina (who is from Cuba) talk and drink coffee in front of the television. We stay until all Spanish programs are over for the evening.

As soon as we return to our apartment, Pepin and I cannot help ourselves, and we start running around the empty space. "Okay, that's enough, time to go to bed!"

Nena yells. Pepin grabs a comic book and starts reading in his own bed. I fall asleep, sucking on my middle finger and gently tapping Nena's cheek, my self-comforting habit, while she fills in letters to the *Vanidades* crossword puzzle.

Shame—P.S. 173

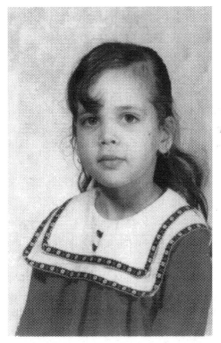

Nelly's first grade picture

I am sitting quietly in my first-grade class, scissors in hand, cutting and pasting. My heart begins to thump as my mother walks in un-expectantly. She's wearing a trench coat. I notice the lace of her nylon pajamas underneath, and with *chancletas* rapidly flapping, she goes up to my teacher, Ms. Specter, who gets up to meet this intruder.

Nena says, "I an heeeaaa, I Nelly's mother, you letter say I need to con."

"Oh yes." Ms. Specter smiles. "You missed the parent-teacher conference . . . let's go to the hallway to talk," and Ms. Specter signals for me to join them. Ms. Specter says, "Nelly is a wonderful girl. She's always prepared, so well behaved, and one of my top readers. She is an excellent student and a pleasure to have in class." Ms. Specter looks at me lovingly, like she does when she brings me clothes. As Ms. Specter spoke, Nena was jingling her keys, avoiding the teacher's gaze, and sucking on her teeth.

My mother puts her face right up against Ms. Specter's and says, "Is that it? Is that what you want to tell me?" Ms. Specter's face goes from polite, social smile to puzzlement. "You made me con heeeaaaa to tell me dat? I an a waitress, and when I don't work, I dons get paid!"

By now, my mother's voice is so loud, other teachers have come out of their classrooms ready to subdue and restrain this crazy Dominican. She continues screaming, "I know she a good girl! I know she do her ho-work! I know she an excellent student!"

She pulls me toward the exit of the school, yelling, "*Coñaso, estos comemierdas haciendo la gente pasar trabajo por gusto*[These assholes making trouble for me]." She stops in the middle of her rant and points her finger at me. "*Tu vez la baina que yo paso por ustedes*[Look at all I have to go through because of you kids]." She pushes me toward the schoolyard as I hear the all too familiar speech about why did God punish her by making her have children. "*Gran Poder de Dios, quien me mando a parir?*"

Meanwhile, she'd been laid off from work and had been spending most of her days sleeping.

Venetian Blinds

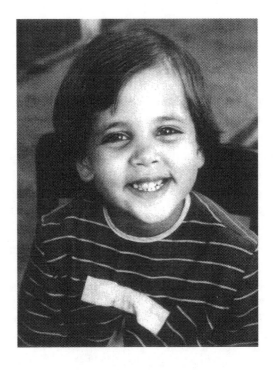

"Walkin through dark, stinky hallways can be hard on anybody, man or chile, but a chile can get snatch in the dark and get his behind parts messed up by some weirdo; I'm talking bout them sexuals. Soon's you get up to leven, twelve and so—they might cool it cause they scared you know where to land a good up—punch, dig? I say alla this cause it's a fact . . ."
—*A Hero Ain't Nothin' but a Sandwich by Alice Childress*

Pepin and I are sleeping together on our twin bed. Approximately two feet across from our bed is my mother's twin bed. Tonight a violent sound wakes us from a deep sleep. My mother is lying in bed with her rollers on in her hair, with a man. They're both naked. He's on top, and she's just lying there with the rollers rocking along a pillow as he violently thrusts himself repeatedly onto her.

Both Pepin and I sit up and stare. He is seven years old. I am six. Pepin puts his arm around my shoulders and cradles me back to sleep, burying my face into his neck.

"Shh," he whispers. "It's okay, just don't look." I suck on my finger, and my brother kisses my forehead. The thumping of the other twin bed continues, and I fall asleep.

This same person, Cuco, who I see pushing onto my mother, wakes me from a deep sleep. He is on top of me. I am shocked without knowing what to do, so I do what my mother did—I just lay there. I turn my face toward Pepin, who is lying right beside me, and I try to speak, but my mouth is frozen. There is no physical pain involved, just a rubbing sensation. I close my eyes until it ends.

Nena is lying on one of the twin beds in our bedroom. Cuco has a robe on and signals me to follow him to the living room. He turns toward the window, pulls the cords of the Venetian blinds to close upward, and then downward, and then decides to leave them closed facing upward. He lays himself down on the splintered wooden floor and motions me to come over to him.

He holds me up in the air, the way my mother sometimes holds us up when we play Superman, pretending that we are flying. He is looking at my body, which is parallel to his. He is wearing glasses, he has dark brown skin, and his hair is balding.

Nena yells, "*Nelita, que tu haces* [Nelita, what are you doing]?" He quickly puts me down, gets up suppressing his laughter, and signals me with his finger over his lips, as if what just occurred a few feet away from my mother is never to be revealed.

I yell back, "Nada, Mommy!" and I run to her side.

"Stay here with me," she says.

(I have no recollection of these moments beyond this.)

A few days later, Pepin's crying awakens me on an early Sunday morning. Cuco did something to him in the bathroom that makes him soil his underwear. Pepin is sitting up in bed, holding his stomach, and when he stops crying, he is staring blankly at the wall. He will not talk. After giving up on trying to make him answer my question, he shows me his soiled underwear. He finally says, "He did it to me, and now my stomach hurts."

Cuco fondles me when no one else is around. He bathes me. He bought me new panties once and played with the crotch as he folded each one, put it in my drawer, and smiled at me. He received magazines wrapped in a brown paper bag, and when we were alone, he sat me on his lap, opened the package, and showed me the dirty pictures. There was one picture of a little girl completely naked on a swing. He made me watch as he put his penis onto this picture.

Whenever he is near me, I become paralyzed with fear. I never fight back. I never tell anyone what he does to me.

Sometime later, Nena tells Pepin and me to go to Rosalina's apartment next door. We hear our apartment door opening and closing several times, and we go back to see what's going on. A row of brown paper shopping bags are lined up against the hallway wall. My mother is sitting on the bed crying uncontrollably while the disgusting man, Cuco, packs his things in the paper bags. We run back to Rosalina to tell her what's going on and then return to our apartment. No adult is speaking. At one point, my mother goes to the bathroom and swipes a collection of men's colognes from a small glass shelf onto the floor.

"*No te olvides tus perfumes, siempre tan preocupado de como hueles* [Don't forget your bottles of perfume, you who is always so concerned with how you smell]."

51

My Seventh Birthday Party, 1969

I am having a party for my seventh birthday because Nena says that in Dominican tradition, seven is an important year to celebrate. Rosalina, my next-door neighbor, sewed a dress for me as my present. It is made of pink satin with shimmery sleeves. The morning of the party, the house is cleaned, furniture rearranged for open space in which to dance. Streamers are crisscrossing the ceiling, and the kitchen table, now moved to the living room, is decorated with a pastel paper table cover and a two-tiered cake.

   "*Mamí, el viene, verdad* [Mom, he's coming, right]?" Pepin asks my mother.

"*Sí, Pepín, lo llame, y el dijo que venía* [Yes, I called him, and he said he was coming]," my mother answers him. As I focus on the decorations, an apartment soon to be filled by people and the opening of the presents afterward, I have nothing but complete, overwhelming excitement. I walk around the house with a new grin I've invented just for today. I curl my upper lip inwards and scrunch my whole face with a wide grin.

My brother, helping with the cleaning and rearranging of the furniture, asks me, "Do you think Carlito will come?"

I answer, "Eeeeeee! I think everyone we called is coming."

We start skipping do-c-do style, alternating lock-in arms. "I can't wait to see Papi. Mami said he's coming," says Pepin.

"Eeeeeeeee!" I squeal and start running around again.

I'm ready for the guests. I have on my new dress and a paper crown on my head. The anticipation is too much, so I lean over the window and stare at the courtyard, waiting for my guests to arrive. "Hi!" I yell at three friends who are sisters and wearing chiffon dresses and salon style hairdos. "I'll ring the bell to let you in the building." I run to the staircase, grab the hand of the youngest, drag her into my living room where Johnny Ventura merengue is blasting, and start dancing with her. I stop abruptly to look out the window and wait for more guests. The three sisters join me, and when another guest arrives in the courtyard, we all start yelling, "Come up! It's here! Come up!" I run to ring the bell, run toward the stairs to greet them, pull them into my living room to dance. "Mommy, I want the song 'Sugar Sugar'!" I yell.

Pepin answers, "I got it, Nelly."

The party is now in full swing, and the apartment is full of people. The small ham sandwiches have been eaten, and near empty cups of soda are everywhere. Some children and adults are dancing. Other kids have broken up into makeshift games. A group is playing roller derby in the hallway (sliding with socks instead of roller skates), another set of girls are using their dresses to slide down the steps, and still others are venturing into neighbors' apartments. My mother tries to gather the group together. "Time to cut the cake!" she yells.

"No, no, no, not until Papi gets here!" Pepin cries out. "And, Mommy, I've been thinking, I haven't had a birthday party." He starts crying, goes to our bedroom, and slams the door shut.

"*Nena, ese niño necessita un psychiatra, te lo estoy diciendo* [Nena, I'm telling you, that boy needs to see a psychiatrist]," my mother's cousin advises her.

"*Una Buena pela es lo que necessita* [A good beating is what he needs]," my mother answers loud enough for Pepin to hear. "*Salte del cuarto coño, y deja tu vagamundería* [Get out of the room and stop your fooling around]!" my mother yells as she's about to grab my brother and bring him out to be present for the cake cutting.

Luis, a neighbor, witnesses this and decides to offer comfort by telling Pepin not to worry, he's going to get him a cake. Luis's nickname was Jerry Lewis, both for the striking resemblance to the famous actor and for his sense of humor. The past Christmas, Luis surprised us with toys and warmed up the day by organizing an impromptu Christmas party in his studio apartment. "*Nena, no empieces cantar 'happy birthday' hasta que yo vuelva con el biscocho de Pepín*," he tells my mother, who agrees to wait.

Back to dancing, running, roller derby, trying to climb onto the fire escape, looking through my mother's makeup drawer, the chaos that an unstructured apartment party is supposed to be in all of its glory.

When Luis returns, all the kids gather around him, and he lifts the cake over his head as the crowd is impeding his movement. We're jumping up and down yelling, "Here's the cake!" Luis sets up Pepin's cake on the convertible sewing machine. He's even remembered a separate paper birthday tablecloth.

We now have a two-person birthday party, and before the crowd sings "Happy Birthday" to me around my table, we're going to take pictures. Our pose, Nena in the middle, Pepin leaning against her right hip with her arm around him, and me up on a chair on my mother's left side. As the picture is taken, I revert to the new smile for the day, and Pepin is sulking. "Where's my Pops?" The party continues. I am in absolute bliss, running from person to person, activity to activity. Big eyes full of tears, Pepin cuts his cake after being sung "Happy Birthday."

It's past midnight when we say good-bye to the last guests, and I am reenergized with the thought that now I get to open my presents. I giggle and squeal after unwrapping a psychedelic flip-open box that holds 45 rpm records. I turn to show it to Pepin, but he is looking out the window, crying quietly, waiting for our Pops. We haven't heard from Angel in months. Pepin waits by the window, hoping to catch a glimpse of him.

Pepin is always waiting for Papi. Pepin runs to the phone, hoping it's Pops on the line. Pepin writes Pops letters begging him to come see us. Pepin talks about our father as if we had an arranged custody agreement that included regular visits. He tells our friends about all the things we're going to do when our Pops visits. "He's taking me to the Mets versus the Pirates game." "I'll ask my Pops to see if he could coach Little League this summer." "I don't know if I can come over next weekend. My Pops will most probably pick me up."

Angel Maseda does show up every once in a while. On those visits, the day for us feels like Christmas, our birthdays, and Happy New Year all at once. Angel brings us joy, especially Pepin, who is in a blissful state when he's with his father. The last time our Pops came, he took us to Hobbyland toy store and then for banana milkshakes at his favorite diner in the Bronx, where the waitress brings the blender over to our table and we get to see the bananas churn until they disappear. Pepin doesn't let go of him during the visits. When the time for Angel to leave arrives, Pepin starts crying and begging, "I want to come live with you."

"Yes, my *lindo*, you will one day. When I move to Puerto Rico, you're coming with me," Angel answers.

"Papi, I can't wait," Pepin says as he starts to calm down.

At the end of this party, Pepin is crying because my father didn't show up. He's trying to be quiet while he sobs. He knows the more he cries for his father, the worse will be the beating Nena will give him. She reaches now for him angrily.

"*Coño, muchacho, callate la boca ya* [Boy, shut your mouth already]." She cannot handle Pepin's longing for his father, his depressive moods. She's now ranting about how she does everything for him, but it's only his father he wants. Nena pulls his hair. "*Que te muevas de esa ventana maricon* [Move from the window, you faggot]!" she screams as he claws at the window frame, refusing to let go. She slaps him across the face. "*Te voy a poner a dormir caliente esta noche* [You are going to sleep nice and warm tonight]," a reference to the beating he's going to get if he doesn't stop crying. She starts beating him, and he escalates to screams.

That night, I fall asleep with Pepin in his bed. We're hugging, and he quietly whispers in my ear, "I hate her so much! I want my Pops." We fall asleep with our arms wrapped around each other.

Find Someplace to Go

Nelly third grade school picture

"Every day and every hour, every minute, walk round yourself and watch yourself, and see that your image is a seemly one. You pass by a little child, you pass by, spiteful, with ugly words, with a wrathful heart; you may not have noticed the child, but he has seen you, and your image, unseemly and ignoble, may remain in his defenseless heart. You don't know it, but you may have sown an evil seed in him and it may grow, and all because you were not careful before the child, because you did not foster in yourself a careful, actively benevolent love. Brothers, love is a teacher; but one must know how to acquire it, for it is hard to acquire, it is dearly bought, it is won slowly by long labor. For we must love not only occasionally, for a moment, but forever. Everyone can love occasionally, even the wicked can."

—*The Brothers Karamazov* by Dostoyevsky

One cold Sunday afternoon, I am walking along Audubon Avenue with Nena and her new man. We go into a grocery store where she and he select a small, dirty Spanish-language magazine called *LUZ*. They look at the pictures of naked people, read the text, and I pretend to decide between Cheese Doodles and Lays potato chips. His hand reaches into her coat, they kiss, he pays for the magazine. As we start to walk back toward our apartment, Nena turns to me and says, "Can't you find somewhere to go?"

I'm eight years old, and I don't know where Pepin is. He knows the streets well and would know what to do right now. These activities of Nena with men frighten me. I learned from Pepin and his friends about sex, where babies come from, and what is forbidden. References to the private parts and what men and women do together is dirty.

My secret is that I am also dirty. I am silent about what I already know about sex and ashamed because a stranger rubbing against me is sex. I know that parts of our bodies are supposed to be unseen and untouched. I have already been touched that way and feel unworthy. When people tell me what a good girl I am, I feel guilty, as if I've committed a crime. This secret, I feel, I can never tell anyone about.

I sometimes hear Nena brag to her friends, "If any man touches my little girl, I'll kill him with my bare hands." I believe her, but I also ask myself, *If that's the way you feel, why did you leave me alone in the apartment with a stranger? Why did you let him give me a bath? Am I to blame?* Nena always claims that "men are dogs, and they'll bark up any tree." They are primitive animals who "cannot control themselves once the sexual urge arises." So why allow me near these men? The only explanation is that I somehow am to blame. Furthermore, I know even as a small child that this secret is a burden I cannot unload on my beloved Pepin, who probably has been violated himself or certainly saw me being violated. Where is our father? I need him too.

My sadness is made worse by the biting cold and the howling wind against my face as I turn south on Audubon Avenue. She and he go north. I head toward 171st and Amsterdam Avenue to my grandmother's apartment. "*Y Nena, adonda esta* [Where is Nena?]?" my grandmother asks.

"She's home, Mama. I came here because I wanted to be with you," I say as I hug the little seventy-three-pound woman when she greets me at her door. I never talk about the men who visit Nena. There are some friends and even relatives that do not pass up the opportunity to humiliate Mama, Pepin, Gilbert or me by telling us that my mother is a whore. My grandmother is pure love. I cannot bring myself to tell her at this moment where her daughter is and what she is doing.

"*Nelita, tienes hambre* [Are you hungry]?" Mama asks.
"*No, Mama, adonde esta Ochie?*"

Mama and I go next door where Ochie, my cousin, is. These neighbors are having a Sunday gathering with food, laughter, music, and games. I've just met this family, and I'm in their apartment, comfortably sitting on the floor, and eating their food, and they immediately like me. "*Que Linda con esos ojos verdes* [Look at those beautiful green eyes]!" the mother remarks.

My new friends want me to participate in their family rally, and for some inexplicable reason, for the few hours I'm in this apartment, they want to take care of me. The oldest child asks me to sleep over, and Mama answers, "Why would she sleep here, having me next door?" They're fighting over me.

But it's becoming dark out, and I need to go home to prepare for school tomorrow. I take St. Nicholas Avenue back up to 176th Street since it is more populated, and I'm scared to walk home alone. I notice a man with a thick, black mustache walking behind me. I try to be inconspicuous as I look back at him periodically to see if he's still there. I quicken my pace. Fear is taking hold of me. During one of my back glances, I see that his penis is visible outside of his un-zipped pants. I hug myself as I add an occasional skip. Now I'm walking so fast I'm almost running. Finally, 176th Street. I hope a neighbor is looking out of the window should anything happen.

I run up to the front door of my building. I don't have to ring the buzzer to my apartment because I see a neighbor, Mamia, through the glass pane standing in the lobby. The man in arctic gear is standing about ten feet away from me with his penis out, as if having his penis exposed in twenty-degree Fahrenheit is natural. As Mamia opens the door, he walks away, and Mamia says "*Mi Nina, que te pasa* [My girl, what's the matter]?"

"Nothing, it's just that it's so cold outside." She takes me into her apartment. I sit on her couch while she starts gossiping about who's coming in and who's going out. I'm still shaking from the thought I might have been kidnapped and raped and hope Mamia doesn't notice my state of shock.

I don't want to leave her apartment to go upstairs. She's already told me that the Archillas, in whose apartment I'm always welcomed and have stayed in for days, have been out all day and haven't returned. I calculate the right amount of time before I'm impolite to just hang out here. Orestes, one of the Cuban *boliteros*, comes in. "*Mamia, que me cuentas? Nelita, como estas?*" I guess I can stay a little longer. When Orestes leaves, I leave with him. He insists on walking me upstairs, and I'm relieved. He sees me safely to my landing, turns around, and goes back down. I knock, and Nena opens the door. I run into our room, and she goes into the living room.

Tonight, I don't have to share my twin bed with Nena because she'll be entertaining in the living room. Tonight, I will miss pressing my body against hers, watching her do the crossword puzzles from the *Vanidades* magazine. I prepare for bed, and finally Pepin comes home around 10:30. He's smiling when he first walks in, telling me how he spent the day at an abandoned building with friends, making treasure-hunt discoveries. His face drops, and his large, bulging eyes sadden when he realizes the sleeping arrangement for the night—a new man. At least she's moved this activity to the living room.

Pepin starts talking about our Pops. "I know he's going to call this week, Cuqui [his nickname for me], and when he asks us what we want to do on this visit, let's tell him ice skating at Rockefeller Center." And so we fall asleep as we plan this idyllic outing. While Pepin fantasizes about activities with our father that never come to be, I fantasize about being just like Mary Tyler Moore. This new television show I started watching, now in 1970, portrays the single, independent, professional woman I want to grow up to be.

Gilbert Arrives

"It's ten p.m. Do you know where your children are?" This public service announcement always scares me when it comes on and Pepin is not home. He is beginning to spend more and more time hanging out on the streets, and I like to have him home by the time we settle in to watch *La Bruja Maldita*, which starts at ten p.m. When I am outside playing with him, he sends me home around seven o'clock, giving himself the privilege of staying out as long as he wants. I obey him, but I wish he would spend more time at home, more time with me instead of with his friends going places where I am not allowed.

Pepin introduced me to one of the hangouts he and his friends discovered, the public library on 179th Street. Here they spend hours looking at pictures of naked ladies. They search for medical books, art books, books on native tribes from far-off places, anywhere pictures of the naked female body can be found. Pepin has filled several composition books copying, mostly, the female nude during his time there. His friends beg to borrow these notebooks so they can stare at the drawings when they are by themselves and admire his works of art. Even Nena and her friends comment on the technical merit of Pepin's artwork.

While Pepin went off with his friends, I remained in the section of the library Pepin instructed me I was not allowed to leave, the area for grammar-school students.

The librarian helped me to choose books appropriate to my reading level. I obtained a library card with Nena's signature forged by Pepin and borrowed books frequently. My favorites were biographies. Queen Elizabeth I, Eleanor Roosevelt, and Leonardo Da Vinci are some of the fascinating figures that I got to know. By reading about these important people in our history, these great achievers, I felt closer to the possibility that maybe I too could someday achieve something great. I was proud to know that Althea Gibson first picked up a tennis racket and played on the courts by the Hudson River. That Maria Callas walked the same streets of Washington Heights as I had. I was inspired by the persistence of Helen Keller to communicate with others. This library gave me the material that satisfied my appetite for what became my refuge—reading a good book.

On one of these nights, Pepin was home early, and we were watching television together. Every once in a while, he would have to get up from the twin bed, reposition the wire hanger we used as an antenna, and slap and kick the TV when the image began to swerve or the thick black lines made rapid runs through the screen. This usually worked to get the image steady again. We fought incessantly over what to watch. Pepin always wanted a sporting event, while I wanted *Mary Tyler Moore* or a variety show. Nena usually let him get his choice as a way of keeping him home.

Tonight, Pepin is doing his usual, acting as a sports announcer and describing the stats of each ball player. I am reading while he goes on and on, and I look at the screen when he insists I have to see an instant replay. I've learned to tune out everything around me while absorbed by a book. Nena is in the kitchen reading her Kabala numerology, interpreting dreams for signs of a possible winning number, when all of a sudden we hear her scream, "*Mi hijo!*"

We turn around and see that a tall, skinny, black guy with a huge Afro has walked into our apartment through the unlocked door. He is wearing a dashiki shirt, very high platform shoes, and is smiling. I panic, thinking we're going to be robbed, but my mother runs up to him and starts hugging and kissing him repeatedly, yelling, "*Mi hijo!*" It was my brother Gilbert, who had returned from the Dominican Republic where we had left him years earlier after Nena and Angel got divorced.

Pepin and I run to him, each grab a leg, and the four of us are jumping up and down with joy. Gilbert arrived with no prior warning and just told us he's here because he wants to be with his Mom. "*Gilbertico, y ese estilo que te haz tirado* [What's this style of yours)?" Nena asks. He explains he's been making trips to the Bahamas where he has connected with his black American brothers. He arrived from the Dominican Republic without the look of a new immigrant; instead he was wearing the latest fashion and had discovered Black Power.

Within a week, Nena had enrolled him at our local high school, George Washington. They showered each other with affection, went shopping together, and Nena proudly repeated to our friends how people in the street mistook her and Gilbert as boyfriend and girlfriend.

The honeymoon between Nena and Gilbert ended after a few months. Hugs and kisses were be replaced by "Don't you think you're just going to lie around here all day, you lazy son of a bitch." Gilbert was fifteen years old and supposed to be going to school, but instead, we had to hear Nena yelling, "I'm sick and tired of you sleeping all day! I've already been called by George Washington High School, and they're ready to kick your black ass out of there. *Estoy harta de ti. Ya vete* [I'm getting tired of you. I want you to leave]."

One night, I hear Gilbert yell at Nena, "*No toque mis cosas* [Don't touch my stuff]!" It is a new fight between them. "*Esa baina no la entres en mi casa* (Don't bring that junk into my home)." Nena rips open a thin aluminum square and flushes the white powder inside of it down the toilet. I close the bedroom door as their violent struggle continues. After these encounters, he leaves for days, usually staying with Mama and Neida. At other times, he simply disappears for weeks at a time, causing fear for his safety among my family.

Not long after one of these fights, I wake up to hear Gilbert yelling from the hallway outside our door. "*Me voy cuando se vaya ese hombre de mi casa* [I'll leave when the man in there leaves my house]!" Pepin and I each have a twin bed to ourselves, which means that Nena is in the living room with one of her boyfriends. This latest one is a Peruvian doctor. Earlier in the evening, she was laughing as he injected her buttocks with penicillin in front of us. Now Gilbert is creating a scene in the middle of the night. He is outside our door holding a chain and a rock the size of a basketball, ready to attack Nena's lover. A neighbor is trying to negotiate a peaceful resolution to this situation. I jump in bed with Pepin for comfort as this scenario plays out. We hear a loud *kaboom*, and the startle makes us hold each other tight. It was the sound of the rock Gilbert had thrown out of the hallway window as it hit the pavement below. The neighbor, Pino, had convinced Gilbert to get rid of the rock and calm down in his apartment. Pino made sure this man would leave our apartment as long as Gilbert did not become violent. When the coast was clear, the Peruvian doctor ran out of our building so fast, he was still pulling up his pants while running out of the courtyard.

This was the end of the pervert parade for the rest of my childhood.

It was replaced by Santana music blasting from our living room as an assortment of hippies, Black Panthers, and Vietnam vets regularly congregated there with the door shut. Nena rarely protested, afraid of her own son and knowing they were all getting high in there.

"*Vete para el carajo* [Go to hell]!" Nena is in a fury, throwing Gilbert's clothing out the window. Today is Gilbert's eighteenth birthday, and Nena has been waiting to legally throw him out of her life. A crowd gathers in the courtyard of our building to watch the raining down of Gilbert's belongings. Nena looks like a werewolf; her hair is covering her face as she bends over to pick up more clothing to throw out the window, all the while continuously screaming the reasons why she wants him out. "*Y esta payaseria no lo quierro ver mas* [I never want to see these clown shoes again]." She is referring to a pair of black and silver platform shoes that Gilbert wore with pride when he went out to party.

Pepin and Nelita Separate

I am sitting on Papi's lap, my head pressed against his soft chest. I smell the nicotine as he gently caresses me on the head, comforting me by saying, "Don't cry, my love. We'll see each other soon." I look up at him. His light brown eyes are wide, and behind his wire-framed glasses, I sense a deep sadness. During my previous contacts with my father, of all the emotions he evoked in me, sorrow was never one of them. Exhilaration and nervousness at the prospect of a visit, affection, safety, and admiration are what I remember feeling.

Whenever I got the chance to hug him, longing and love is what I felt as I held him tight enough in an effort to never let him go, hoping this time he would stay and restore our family. Today in this airport, however, I cry more for whatever it is inside of him that is depressing me.

Pepin has been behaving like a proper young man during this entire visit to Puerto Rico, where we have just shared this Christmas and New Year's holiday with our father. Today is January 6, 1974, and at the San Juan airport, a male flight attendant has a microphone in his hand, explaining in English to the passengers the meaning of today's holiday and how Puerto Ricans celebrate *Los Tres Reyes Magos.*

We are waiting for me to board, alone, a flight to New York City. I am leaving behind Pepin to his dream of living with Angel Maseda, who has relocated to Puerto Rico. Pepin reminds me again, "Nelly, take care of Mom. Help out around the house and try to get her to stop smoking." Earlier this week, Pepin snuck in a phone call to Nena and hung up as soon as he heard her voice answering. "Nelly, she sounded weak, like she was sad or maybe sick. As soon as you get home, write me a letter telling me how she's doing. Man, I feel guilty. I feel like she needs me, the man of the house." I never expected this from him. I thought that after landing in Puerto Rico, Pepin would forget about our apartment in New York and concentrate only on all that living with Pops meant: a house with a backyard; finally his own dog; Pops and him watching endless sports games, especially the Mets playing baseball; hours of Pepin and Angel with their catcher's gloves on, pitching a ball to each other on the beach.

Instead, he almost seems to regret his decision to live with Pops. He feels it will be unsafe for Mom and me to be alone. Instead of it being a comfort that Gilbert is in New York, it's another source of stress and fear. Of course, Gilbert would defend us against an outside perpetrator if needed, but he had a violent streak and sometimes beat on Pepin, beat on his own girlfriends, and made gestures many times suggesting he would do the same to Nena. Calls from the police regarding picking up Gilbert from the local precinct were routine, and Pepin feared for the toll it was taking on Mom.

Now that he is free from this, I cannot understand his remorse. Now that he no longer has to face Nena's rage and her abusive and humiliating behavior toward him, it is guilt that he is feeling.

I listen to both of them lecture me on how to behave, to do well in school, and my father repeats a lesson he has given me at every meal. "First you eat the meat, the most nutritious part of your plate, then the rice and beans." He hated how skinny I was and became impatient when I barely ate from the large portions of food he served. "I'm going to get a *cuatro* made for you, and when you come back, I'll have one of my friends teach you how to play it," Angel promised. (Angel never gave me *el cuatro*.)

"*Abreme la Puerta, abreme la Puerta, abreme compay, abreme la Puerta, lo le lo le lo, lo le lo lay,*" I sing, strumming my imaginary *cuatro*. The three of us laugh, remembering *las trullas Patronales* we enjoyed during this wonderful Christmas vacation. Pepin and I love this tradition we just experienced for the first time—not sleeping in order to serenade your friends in the middle of the night during the holidays. Then the three of us began, "*Y venía la briza y FUA, y me la apagaba*—" interrupted by the overhead speaker in the airport.

The unaccompanied children are asked to board. Angel squats to hug me. Pepin is holding me tightly from behind and says, "I'm going to miss you, Nell. I don't know when I'll see you again." Angel wipes the tears from my eyes and gives me the white, cotton handkerchief from his pocket. I love the smell of cigarette as I use it to blow my nose.

Back in New York, Nena and I each sleep in our own twin bed. When Gilbert shows up, he sleeps on the high rise in the living room. As long as the threat of Gilbert exists, Nena does not bring boyfriends into our home.

Letters and pictures of Pepin arrive in the mail regularly. He is always smiling, and along with the descriptions he writes, we see him with his bike, his dog, his baseball uniform on. He attends a private school with the children of Roberto Clemente, and while at a party with Pops, who has kept in touch with his Latino friends in the music industry, he had a chance to meet Iris Chacon. We received a picture of Pepin with this famous *vedette* whom we grew up watching on Spanish television. When I hear his voice during our occasional phone calls, Pepin is always animated, laughs easily, and emphasizes how great it is to have his own bedroom. Only one thing prevents this time with Angel from being idyllic—Pops's girlfriend, the singer Miriam Alonso, who lives with them. Pepin is jealous of this relationship and prays for their breakup. Despite this, he is living the happiest days of his life.

Another letter arrives from Puerto Rico. Nena opens it, and while reading, she yells, "No!" and I see her start to cry. I am gripped by fear that something terrible happened to Pepin. My mother does not know this, but once, while swimming in Isla Verde Beach in Puerto Rico, I almost drowned. Pepin and I had been left alone by Angel on a stretch of beach with no lifeguard. At one point, Pepin went off by himself and warned me not to go into the water without him. After a while, however, boredom and the intense heat convinced me to go for a swim. Suddenly, while splashing around, I was overcome by the undertow. I lost control of my legs, and my feet cycled their way toward the deep ocean. I tried to scream, but every time I opened my mouth, I swallowed water instead. Underwater, I swam with all my might toward the surface, breathed in a gulp of air, but instantaneously was engulfed back into the chaos of rumbling water pulling me deeper. I was panicking when out of nowhere, it seemed, Pepin lifted me and threw me toward the shore. He repeated this until I made it out of the water. I was coughing and terrified, and a man and woman came over to make sure I was all right. Pepin had earlier met this couple who took him on a boat ride. It was from there that Pepin saw me drowning, caught in the deadly tunnel of water. The terror of that incident remains a palpable feeling that I often relive. Now that I see my mother convulsed in pain as she reads this letter, my heart is thumping at the thought that Pepin drowned in these same waters.

I grab the letter from her hands, and Nena continues sobbing over the kitchen table. An unbuttoned sweater over her hunched shoulders made her seem very old at that moment. My eyes quickly fell on a word written in all capital letters: CANCER. I start the letter from the beginning, trying to concentrate despite my trembling hands shaking the paper, and learn that Angel Maseda was informing Nena that Pepin would have to return to New York after completing this academic year. Angel was becoming too sick to care for Pepin. I read over several times: *"Me voy a morir de CANCER, tengo cancer de los pulmones* [I am going to die of cancer, I have cancer of the lungs)," Angel announces.

Crying, Nena says *"Por eso es que, Nelita, tu viste esa tristeza en el"* [That is why you saw the sadness in him]." Our next-door neighbor Rosalina comes over after hearing our voices. Rosalina holds my head with both of her hands, closes her eyes, and calls on spirits as she starts to pray. She has told me I have the highly evolved spirit of an African who is protecting me, and she is calling for it to make its presence known now. We keep our silence as she continues her *espiritismo* incantations for us.

Pepin returns to New York after the school year ends. When we pick him up at the airport, he is wearing a suit and tie and insists on carrying his own bags. He speaks mainly Spanish now, behaving like a proper young man. His movements are slow, he barely smiles, and I feel his depression. In our apartment, Nena fixes Pepin a pastrami sandwich on rye, and after slowly chewing one bite, he looks at me with his large eyes and says, "I can't eat." Nena kisses him, tries to loosen his tie, but Pepin gets up and walks into the living room, disregarding her attempts. I follow him. He sits on our plastic-covered couch and stares straight ahead toward the wall with his hands on his knees.

"Peps, let's go outside. Everyone is waiting to see you" I try to animate him. I feel a lump in my throat; his sadness overwhelms me.

"No, Nell, not now," he responds. His large, sad eyes do not cry, and he remains in this position for hours, staring straight ahead of him.

The next academic year at P.S. 143, Pepin started out doing well, but he began having difficulties as the year wore on. "Nelly, I don't know what's happening to me," he tells me as I'm getting ready for school one morning. I woke up to find him sitting on the high rise, biting his knuckles. "I haven't slept all night, and right now, I feel really nervous. Look at my hands." He shows me how he is shaking, and I see red, scaly marks left by his teeth on his hands. "But I don't know why," he says in an agitated voice. I feel so sorry for Pepin. I cannot help him, Nena won't help, and I have to get to school.

Nena began getting notices from school. *Jose Maseda, one of my brightest students, is now struggling to pass . . . Jose Maseda seems distracted, unable to concentrate . . . Jose Maseda is not meeting his potential and seems to be giving up on his schoolwork.* This triggered a verbal tirade from Nena, whose emotional abuse against Pepin took a turn toward the sadistic.

"You're a god-damned failure. You are going to be a nobody. I'm getting sick of watching you throw your life away. All you do is sleep all day and watch television all night and hang out with your friends. I can't even have visitors to this house because of the smell of urine coming from the high rise . . ." These became some of her daily verbal assaults on him.

During one of those confrontations, Pepin grabbed Nena by her shirt collar, and with the other hand, he aimed a dumbbell weight at her face. This fight occurred because Neida and other visitors were present when Nena started yelling that she could not offer to have them sit in the living room due to the stench of urine. This public humiliation of Pepin for his inability to control his bladder while he slept provoked him. We all held our breaths as we watched this potential tragedy. Nena's eyes were wide open with fear as she stared at Pepin in his fury, expecting the weight to be smashed against her face. He finally throws the dumbbell on the floor, lets go of Nena, and walks out of the apartment. "Get him a psychiatrist, Nena. Your son is not well." But Nena answers her friend's warning with her usual response.

"What he needs is a good beating and then to be thrown out of this apartment."

Pepin managed to finish that academic year, graduate from eighth grade, and go to George Washington High School—a school notorious for violence, chronic underachievement, and its very high dropout rate, our brother Gilbert being one of those dropouts.

October of 1975, I come home one day from school and go to the kitchen to fry myself two eggs. I hear Nena come in. She has a letter in her hands and is crying uncontrollably. "*Se murió Angel* (Angel died)," she manages to say. I kneel down in front of her and hold her. Sitting on a kitchen chair, she is losing control of her emotions.

She's talking out loud while sobbing, and there is one phrase she says that sticks in my mind. "*Todos esos hombres y era otro Angel que yo buscaba* [All those men, and it was another Angel I was looking for)." This strikes me because she has never acknowledged what has been such a source of resentment between Nena and her children—that is, the men she brings home.

The letter in her hand is from the Social Security Administration, informing her of the monthly $330 benefit checks Pepin and I would each be receiving as a result of Angel Maseda's death. This is how we found out our father died.

I leave her after we've both cried together awhile, and I go to the corner where Pepin hangs out to give him this news. When I find him, he's with friends and our cousin Ochie, but before I say anything to him, he sees that I've been crying and says, "The old man died, right?" We hug, and he says he needs to be alone.

Ochie holds my hand and says, "Let's go tell Mama."

I bury my face into the neck of my beloved grandmother and give her the news. Mama gets up, stretches her arms up above her, and screams, "*Gran poder de Dios, esto sí va a matar Nena y Pepin* [Great God, this will kill Nena and Pepin]!"

Two Paths

Nelita at Aquinas

Pepin Spinning Records

Sister Joan Davis calls out my name during tenth-grade Biology, and I freeze with fear. "Nelly, I want to talk to you after class," she says.

I nod back affirmatively and begin thinking, *What did I do wrong? I just won first place in the science contest, I get nineties or a hundred on all of my tests, I never miss a day of school . . .* I start to meticulously think of every step I've taken every day in this class and anxiously ask myself repeatedly, *What could it be?*

Maybe it was the day I was scraping the Petri dishes with bacteria as Ms. Mangialardi guided me, I think to myself. Ms. Mangialardi teaches Regents Biology for the more advanced students. She mentored me for the science project I thought of and then entered into the science competition. My idea was to test common household cleaners whose labels claim to kill bacteria, to see if in fact they do kill common bacteria. Sister Joan Davis, upon hearing of my idea, encouraged me to pursue this project for the upcoming science contest. She brought in a catalogue from which agar-filled Petri dishes and vials filled with different germs could be purchased. We read labels, such as "coliform bacteria" and "anaerobic bacteria." I then had to look up in biology reference books which of these bacteria are common inhabitants and which have the potential to cause human disease.

After the package arrived, I set a date after school with Ms. Mangialardi to prepare my science project. The different bacteria arrived as a gel filling just the bottom of each test tube, labeled with the species name, such as E. coli. The small, round Petri dishes were filled with agar, a substance used to grow bacteria. The first step of this experiment was simple: heat each test tube until the congealed bacterial mixture liquefied. I then inserted a sterile, thin metal rod with a loop at the end of it into the liquid. I proceeded to smear the agar with the end loop covered in broth, forming triangles as I broke the agar up into thirds.

After covering each dish, I labeled which bacteria was growing in it, such as E. coli, Streptococcus, etc. I placed all twenty-five Petri dishes in a warm incubator to let the bacteria grow. I checked them daily, waiting for visible bacterial colonies. Once the separate triangles showed the dots of germs, we were ready for the next step.

To each dish with its separate triangle of microbes, I then added different brand-name "anti-bacterial" cleaners. I then reincubated the dishes, and in forty-eight hours, I had my answers. Some bacterial colonies had been cleared, and others were unaffected by these common household cleaners that advertised themselves as anti-bacterial, thus proving that not all of these detergents actually killed household germs as they claimed.

To put into practice what we were learning in class about microorganisms was such a thrill to me. An awakening occurred, that I could understand science and its application to the real world. That I came up with an idea, and that this idea was taken seriously by my teachers, who took time out of their schedules to see me through this experiment, was a very special experience for me.

Now, why does Sister Joan Davis want to talk to me? Was I too arrogant? Was I disrespectful to her or Ms. Mangialardi? Did I forget to thank someone?

The bell rings for the end of this period, and I meet with Sister Joan Davis, who says to me, "Nelly, I saw your choice of classes for junior year. Bookkeeping, Typing—why aren't you taking Regents Chemistry"?

"With these classes, I can get a job right after high school," I reply, sensing a change of plans is in the works for me.

"Nelly, you have so much potential. You can be whatever you want to be in life—an astronaut, a teacher, a doctor. I see college in your future, and you had better rethink this schedule for next year. You are my top student, and I urge you to go the academic track."

I loved this school. At a time during the 1970s when the Bronx was literally burning down, violent gangs spreading terror and its streets as dangerous as many war zones, there stood, in the South Bronx, Aquinas High School, my haven. Inside of this building were the most beautiful and dedicated people I have ever met, the Dominican Sisters of Sparkhill and teachers. The building was clean, safe, and orderly. I would walk into it in the morning on shiny wood floors and smell freshly baked Italian rolls. We were met with warm greetings from our teachers and staff, who encouraged us to eat and prepare our brains for a day of learning. As soon as I stepped into this environment, I put the turmoil of my home away.

At the beginning of eighth grade, there were friends of mine whose parents were determined not to send their children to the local public high school in Washington Heights. In 1975, this school, George Washington High School, was in chaos. Open drug dealing, shootings, and teachers afraid of their students characterized what was going on inside of this building. I remember visiting when Pepin, a freshman there, took me during a school day. He and some friends were just hanging out in the lunchroom listening to music and dancing. I even joined in for a few rounds of my favorite activity, dancing the hustle. The bell would ring for change of class, and everyone seemed to ignore it. At some random time, Pepin decided it was the end of the school day for him, and we went home. That was pretty much how he spent his time there until he dropped out.

Some friends of mine were looking into Catholic high schools, and when I became aware of this alternative, I decided I would do the same. One school in particular caught my attention, Aquinas High School. I didn't know where it was located.

What I did know was that the neighborhood girls who were students there were nice and warm. The problem with going to Aquinas was where was I going to get the money?

Nevertheless, I took the Catholic high school entrance exam and was accepted to, Aquinas.

Nena didn't know what was going on with my high school plans. If there was a permission slip to sign, she'd sign it, not concerning herself with the details. I did not raise the money issue with her, as I was just starting eighth grade, and my high school plans were in the theoretical phase. I knew what her answer would be if I mentioned that I wanted to go to private school, the way she always answered when we asked her for money.

"*Pesos no tengo, pero pelos sí* [I don't have dollars, but I have plenty of hairs]," she would say as she pointed to her pubic area.

Then, in October of 1975, we got the letter from the US government informing us of our benefits due to Angel's death. The Social Security income to minors of deceased parents was how I was able to pay my tuition at Aquinas High School. Angel gave me more in death than in life. As sad as it was for me to lose my father, a recurring thought became, *Dad, your timing was great. All those times you'd call, get us excited about coming over to take us out and never show up, leaving Pepin clawing at the windowsill crying, "I know he's coming, this time he's coming." This time, Pops, you came through.*

Every day, I looked forward to going to Aquinas High School. I always had my homework done and redone, obsessively memorizing all of my schoolwork because my sense of gratitude for being in such a wonderful place translated into my becoming a student who would not accept a grade lower than an A. I awoke to a world filled with possibilities. I had never before really thought about my future or had ever seen myself in the light that my teachers portrayed me, as someone with promise.

At home, my brother Gilbert was fully entrenched in his heroin addiction. Pepin periodically spiraled into rages and disrupted sleep cycles that made it impossible for him to continue going to school. Nena would sleep as much as she could until one of us woke her up. Then her day of constant yelling, screaming, and putting down her boys would begin.

My mind, however, was focused on my schoolwork and on my future away from this mayhem.

Yale Interview

"When I met the big men to whom my letters were addressed I would put on my best manner. I would speak softly, in my most polished tones, smile agreeably and be most polite; and I would remember that if he ("he" meant any of the important gentlemen) should begin a topic of conversation (I would never begin a subject of my own) which I found unfamiliar, I would smile and agree. My shoes would be polished, my suit pressed, my hair dressed (not too much grease) and parted on the right side; my nails would be clean and my armpits well deodorized—you had to watch the last item. You couldn't allow them to think *all* of us smelled bad."

—*Invisible Man* **by Ralph Ellison**

It was the fall of 1979, and excitement was overwhelming me, putting me in a permanently good mood at the thought that soon

I would be away, living in a college dorm. The college application process was an exhilarating experience. I embraced every step, from receiving the application in the mail, to reviewing each page of the college catalogue, to envisioning myself as one of the students pictured in those catalogues whose mind was occupied on grander questions, such as "Why do humans have consciousness?" or "How was Galileo able to discern planetary motion without high-powered lenses in the seventeenth century?" I could see myself in a chemistry lab mixing solute into solvent and writing down my findings. Such thoughts and imagery consumed me during this time in my life. Focused on the future, I dreamed of becoming a medical doctor, a profession of helping that would allow me to pursue my love of science.

With the excitement of a small child at the circus, I looked forward to my interview at this most prestigious of institutions. The interview was to take place in the Riverdale section of the Bronx early on a Sunday morning. I wore a brown skirt, a matching brown cowl-neck sweater, and a fake gold necklace carefully placed underneath my collar. I had straightened my long, wavy hair and put on just enough makeup to seem well put together but not overly so. I saw in the mirror a conservative, presentable young woman. I never dressed provocatively, remembering Nena telling me, "Ponte sexy, Nelita," and reflexively doing just the opposite, never wanting to show my sexuality like she would. I always hated that men in our neighborhood felt justified in verbally abusing women as they walked down the street, although to them, the lascivious comments were compliments, *piropos. I am sure the women at Yale would never put up with that kind of nonsense from men*, I thought to myself.

Nena is asleep. It's Sunday morning, and, as usual, my morning routine of readying myself is done without making a sound. God forbid I wake up Bustin Bronco (one of Pepin's nicknames for Nena).

I arrive at the interview and am somewhat surprised by the casual atmosphere. Cushions are strewn on the floor of this apartment, and a very warm, overweight woman with big earrings seems happy to see me. She is the Yale alumna who has read my application and is to interview me. The crowd consists of Yale alumni interviewers and prospective students. Everyone has a drink and a snack in hand and is either talking while standing or sitting on the floor leaning against a cushion. I am now really scared. I don't know what to say. I have no exposure to socializing or making small conversation. Where do I stand? Should I eat? Who is watching me? What do I talk about? I expected a formal setting with a very stiff-appearing, older, grey-haired person looking at me from across a large mahogany desk, interrogating my credentials. Instead I'm supposed to contribute to discussions revolving around my tennis game or lunch at the club.

Rescuing me, the large woman directs me toward the food. "Get something to eat and let's sit and talk," she says. My heart is beating so hard, and my hands shaking uncontrollably. I grab a bagel, but I don't dare eat it. My exhilarating excitement has turned into oppressive anxiety, and I'm just hoping not to trip over one of these cushions and vomit on someone.

I find a spot on the edge of a sofa, close enough to my hostess, who is sitting on the floor cross-legged. I do not want to sit on the floor, too disrespectful, but she cannot interview me while I'm standing. She would have to crane her neck to look up to me. A circle of interviewers and applicants forms around us.

"Why don't we start with your questions. Please ask us what you would like to know about Yale," the lady with big earings states. She is clearly in control as she inspects us with her large, bulging, grey eyes.

"I heard Professor [so and so] is being nominated for the Nobel. I read it in the alumni magazine my father gets," says preppy white man in a suit. I know now I will have absolutely nothing to say to these people. I have no one in the circles of higher education whom I can claim as a relative. I am even more anxious. What am I going to say about my relatives? What do I say if someone asks me what my siblings are planning for their future? My mind is swirling with the fear that these people might find out my mother is running numbers, Gilbert is injecting heroine and mugging people to feed his habit, and Pepin has given up on school, and his rages have almost destroyed all the furniture in our apartment. Ochie has races with his friends about who can steal a car radio the fastest.

"I know that the dorms are coed; does that mean males and females are separated by floor?" asks another prospective student. How did he know to ask this? I just assumed I would be living in an all-female dorm.

"All the dorms are coed, and be prepared to bump into someone of the opposite sex while in the bathroom," she answers as she smiles, swings her earrings, and licks her lips.

A sound makes its way out of my vocal chords when I hear this, even though I am determined to assume my familiar role of staying still, not making a sound, and hoping no one notices me. "Are there any female-only dorms?" I finally manage to articulate.

The grey eyes widen further, and my interviewer's face becomes red with indignation. "Why would a woman want to be in an all-female dorm? Everyone knows that to be a part of real networking, we need to share all spaces with the males, who are still the ones who dominate in our current society. Only when you are in an environment where you are surrounded by people who are different from you can you find out who you really are." She's lecturing me now. Oddly, we studied this biblical paradox in religion class.

"You have obviously not had your moral convictions tested . . ." And she goes on to expound on the feminists ideals being embraced in the 1970s, some of which I am in favor of, such as equal pay for equal work. I could not wholeheartedly embrace the sexual liberation part of this freedom. As I sit apologetically taking this scolding, I assume this feminist was not raped as a child. Nor did she have a pervert putting his hands up her skirt while on her way to school. I am well acquainted with Betty Friedman and the feminist mystique, but I doubt that she spent time pushing men's lecherous hands away from her breasts or was the victim of violence much too prevalent in communities like mine, especially violence against women. I assume my host had parents who loved and protected her, a mother who prepared her for school in the morning. A life where "sexual liberation" did not mean the fear of men violating you.

I am paralyzed while being called insensitive. "What a disservice is being done to young women like you in an all-girl Catholic school," she states, shaking her head in disbelief.

I am not accepted to Yale.

Worse, I don't defend my beautiful teachers at Aquinas High School. I don't give my point of view of what the other side of feminism looks like—the brave nuns of the Dominican Sisters of Sparkhill, who remained in the South Bronx during its low point of the 1970s, when the neighborhood was literally burning down. A period when Jimmy Carter made a visit to us, and even he remarked the area looked like a war zone from another place and time. These women were there to pull us up from falling into the abyss. They were there for me, to give me back my life.

(This paralysis to speak up afflicts me for much of my time in college and medical school and all but cripples me during my pediatric residency.)

Poverty shamed me, especially because I was one of those children described as being born to "Welfare Queens." And the fact that my family members were involved in criminal activity of one form or another further shamed me into silence. I felt that their activities gave me no rights. Who am I to speak up when I myself do not invite anyone who's not from my neighborhood to my apartment, for fear of the risk I'd put them in? My visitor could be attacked by drug addicts in front of my building and then find herself in the middle of an unexpected outburst of rage by my mother or one of my brothers. To stand still, make no noise, smile, look the preppy part as much as I can—this is what I decide to do when encountering white, middle-class America.

Until the time comes when I can safely come out.

Leaving for Cornell

Pepin and Nelita
June 1980

My two vinyl suitcases are packed. My mother and I wheel them back to our apartment after buying them at the local Chinese store on 174th and Broadway. As we walk back home with them, she says, "*Aquí estamos caminando estos perritos* [Here we are walking these doggies]," and we both start laughing. My doggies and I are ready to leave.

My mother is hyper, talking incessantly, making sure I have all I need for my journey from our Washington Heights apartment to the place I've been dreaming of for years, away to college, to Cornell University.

"Do you have toothpaste?" Nena asks as she hands me a big bottle.

"Yes, Mom, I have toothpaste, but why this red liquid?"

"*Forty Malt, necessitas una Buena vitamina para que no te de anemia por alla* [You need a good vitamin so you don't get anemic over there]," she says. I stare at the bottle with a picture of a man's overdeveloped bicep and wonder how I am going to explain this Latino elixir to my new Cornell friends.

My mother has not been involved in this decision-making process. For her, "away to college" is some theoretical place I'd land simply because I deserve it. She cannot be bothered with the details of how one arrives there. The applications came in the mail, and I filled them out and mailed them back to the school if they agreed to waive the application fee. With enthusiasm, I filled out the paperwork that made my dream seem closer, palpable. I spent hours daydreaming of living in a college dorm with people my age, all in pursuit of higher education. I could not wait for that day to come. Looking forward to the college experience kept me happy and hopeful.

A neighbor, Roberto, who recently arrived from Cuba via the *Mariel* boat lift, insists on driving me to the Port Authority bus station. He has only been in this country a few months and already has a station wagon. My family never owned a car. He thinks I've been through enough to arrive at this place in life, and dragging my bags on the A-train is not an appropriate send-off. Through my financial difficulties, he has seen an America where being poor creates many obstacles to enter the world of higher education. "In my country, all of the children get a free education from preschool through college. You are American born, Nelita, and have had to beg for what all the children of this great country should be given freely, a college education," he says.

My mother is fixing my hair with a brush that has a bone handle when she joins this conversation. "*Sí coño*, and this bastard Reagan, if elected, promises more government cuts in social programs because we all need to learn how to 'pick ourselves up by our bootstraps and make it on our own.'" She's so angry now she slams the brush on the dresser and breaks the handle, a piece of which goes flying across the room. "Did he spend a lifetime fighting with the landlord when his bathroom ceiling collapsed? Did he spend a lifetime fighting off the neighborhood perverts who want to hurt your little girl? Did he spend a lifetime picking up his son from the police precinct? I challenge him to live my life for one week and see where his bootstraps end up."

"Mom, pleeeeeease, if you don't stop ranting, you're going to have to stay here while Roberto takes me."

"It's just that every time white boy with a suit goes on television talking about what a child raised poor without a father should do . . . okay, okay, let's go." My mother turns to the statue of her favorite saint, San Juan Bosco, crosses herself, and says "Please bless Cornell University for accepting my baby girl and for the financial aid."

Beaming, I say, "The doggies are pulling me." I quote Hector Lavoe, "*Hacha y Machete, aquí voy como un cohete* [Machete in hand, here I go like a rocket]." We start laughing, and my mom gives me a big kiss on the cheeks.

My brother Pepin is downstairs sitting on the stoop. He's been crying. "I'm so proud of you, Nelly. You're gonna make it. But I'm going to miss you so much, it just hurts," he says to me. We hug tightly for a long time. We've created a scene, and now our neighborhood friends are coming toward us. I'm surprised by his reaction, but I'm so "outta here" that I want him to stop. I just love his hugs and our open display of affection with each other, but right now, all I can think of is landing in my new world. I don't have the frame of mind to comfort and reassure him. I want to see my dorm room, meet new peers, dive into the intellectual community I've been given entry into.

Dry-eyed, I say to Pepin, "I love you more than anything, Peps. I could not have done this without your love and protection."

"You have no one to thank but yourself!" he says. "I love you so much, Nell." He loses his breath because he's crying so hard.

My cousin Ochie wraps his arms around my waist from behind and says, "You're so lucky to be leaving, but Mama, she's been crying about this." His sibling, Alfy and Elizabeth, hug my legs and start to cry.

"Peps, I've really got to go," I say as I jump into the backseat of the station wagon.

Pepin won't come. "I don't want to see that bus pull away." I stare into his big, hazel eyes that are always so sad. He waves good-bye, and then all of my neighborhood friends start waving as the car pulls away. "*Hacha y Machete, aquí voy como un cohete.*" Now the song is stuck in my mind.

Roberto places my bags in the cargo area of the Greyhound bus. At almost the same time, he and my mom ask me, "*Tienes dinero* [Do you have money]?"

"No, not a penny."

Roberto slaps $300 cash into my palm. I kiss them both and board the bus. My mother is searching for me through the bus windows with a look on her face, as if she forgot to tell me something. We wave.

I introduce myself to the person sitting next to me on the bus. He is an African American football player on the same sojourn.

Sandra's Pregnancy

Senior year at Cornell, it seems like all I have had time for this first semester is filling out medical school applications while taking a course load of biology classes, which includes a killer five-credit genetics class. Mapping out the genome of the fruit fly involved going into the lab at any hour in order to count physical traits of successive generations of this rapidly reproducing insect. Color eyes, wing types, and other characteristics needed to be tallied when a new batch from this cohort hatched. It could mean walking to the lab at three o'clock in the morning to put these bugs under the microscope in order to accurately describe traits that were inherited. This information was then put through statistical analysis that would give us a plausible genetic sequence of our respective fruit flies.

I remember walking toward the lab early one morning in the middle of a snowstorm. Looking through the microscope, I kept losing count of how many red eyed versus white eyed Drosophila I had, confusing my data collection. Exhaustion was messing up my perception. This class was a test of physical endurance as much as it was about inheritance patterns and how to calculate these based on the multigenerational appearance of traits.

Now I'm home with Nena and Pepin for Christmas break, and all I can do is sleep, go to Luigis for Sicilian slices, and come back to the apartment to sleep some more. Awakening from one of these naps, I hear Nena and another woman arguing in the bedroom. I had fallen asleep watching television in the living room.

"*Te estoy diciendo que te saques ha ese muchacho* [I am telling you to take that child out]," Nena says.

"*Nelly, yo no me puedo hacer un aborto, yo soy Cristiana* [I cannot have an abortion, I am a Christian]," the other woman responds.

Nena points at her. "*Sí, pero para acostarte con Pepin no fuiste Cristiana, Cristiana cuando te conviene* [Yes, but to sleep with Pepin, you weren't Christian, Christian when it's convenient for you]. You just want to grab him and make him marry you. Let me tell you something, Pepin is not ready to get married, and much less to become a father. Pepin is a very violent man with a lot of problems. You are going to bring a tragedy with this," Nena prophesies.

I walk over toward the voices, and through a crack in the bedroom door, I see that the other woman is Sandra. I am very surprised. Sandra is one of the sweetest, most polite people I have ever met. She is my age, and when her mother, Niza, a neighbor who lives in the same building as us, brought her three daughters from Ecuador (Nena signed the affidavit that made this possible),

Niza had me come over to her apartment to teach her daughters English. I remember the first time I met the oldest of the three, Sandra. She greeted me at the door with a kiss. I responded with a big hug because for years I had been hearing Niza talk about her three girls, how soon they would be in New York, and detail for me all that she was going to do for them. Niza had bought three beautiful twin-sized beds with wooden headboards painted white and pink, as well as decorative comforters with matching pillows and curtains. Decorations I wish I had. I shared in Niza's anticipation for these girls she missed so much and for whom she was saving money from her factory job to bring to New York. "*Al fin nos conocemos* [Finally we meet)," I said.

"*Gracias por venir. Quierres algo de comer o beber* [Thank you for coming. Would you like something to eat or drink]?"

"Yes, peaches. I know your mom always keeps them," I said.

"*Claro.*" Sandra was giggling.

We were both twelve years old when we first met, and I still remember how polite and mature Sandra was. She returned with a small dessert cup sitting on a saucer, with spoon and napkin, all handed to me as if we were playing tea party. This behavior was not common to my friends and me. We usually drank milk straight out of the carton, and ripping open Cheese Doodle bags was how we usually ate our snacks. We never provided this level of service for each other.

Sandra was the kind of girl who stayed mostly at home, helping her mother with chores and avoiding the streets. I never had a cause for disagreement with her, but never a closeness either. So why was she here arguing with my mother? It seemed so bizarre, someone who would be considered my friend, in my house not to visit me, but to enter into a heated dispute with Nena.

I see Sandra is crying. I am shocked when the contents of the conversation are made clear. Sandra is pregnant with Pepin's child. Nena wants her to abort, and the reason given—rare to hear Nena make this admission—is because of Pepin's violent nature and his disturbing behavior in general. His young age, twenty-two, is obviously a problem as well.

There was never even a hint that Pepin had an interest in Sandra. He had many girlfriends and was particularly close to someone else just a few months before when I was last in Washington Heights. I make a move to enter.

Nena says, "Could you believe this mosquito *muerto* said she's *pregnant* with Pepin's kid? I should pull it from right out of your mouth before that child comes into this world to lead a doomed life . . ." On and on Nena went with her nonstop ranting rage.

Nena Visits Me in Medical School

The phone rings, and I am awakened from a nap. My two liter bottles of diet coke are on the floor empty. I drank them while studying for a pharmacology exam I have tomorrow. I'm finding this particular subject—how receptors in the brain work—very difficult to comprehend and as a result have developed severe headaches studying for this class. I must have fallen asleep without realizing it. I answer the phone.

"Nelita, are you going to be home?" It's Nena.

"*Sí, que pasa?*" I answer. This is a rare phone call, and even rarer, she says she's coming over to visit today. I confirm the address and tell her she can get to me via the number twelve bus.

I'm happy to see her as she walks into the apartment but also bracing myself for what could only be bad news; after all, she rarely visits me. She's distracted and unusually quiet. She sits on my bed and lights a cigarette. "Mom, please don't—" She shuts me up with a look and a wave of her arm.

"*Te tengo que decir algo* [I have to tell you something]." I sit quietly, inhaling the smoke that she exhales, watching her carefully tap the ashes into one of the empty bottles she put between her legs. "*Fulano de tal* [My latest boyfriend) has been cheating on me with a woman I just found out has AIDS," and now she begins to give descriptions of the woman. She has a son with whom she lives in an apartment over the bodega on the corner of 176st Street and Nicholas Avenue, etc.

I have had an easy transition into medical school, given my excellent preparation as a premed at Cornell. However, my life is really all about studying during these four years at Albert Einstein College of Medicine in the Bronx. I have found a wonderful circle of friends, and we manage to laugh at the daily lessons that are intense.

"The end stage of every disease is fibrosis. Life's a bitch, and then you fibrose" becomes our existential refrain when beaten down by loads of unending material to memorize. We find time to see classic movies in the village, and with my close friend Nicholas Holliday, who is also an artist, I visit galleries, and he teaches me how to appreciate art. I think of Pepin when I'm with Nick and how I wish Pepin could have found a way to be like Nick who, despite being poor like me, managed to navigate a place for himself as a student and now a graduate of Brown University.

Pepin comes over to check on me periodically now that I'm living in the Bronx (he never came to visit me at Cornell). He brings me furniture he's found discarded in the street that he has sanded and painted. Pepin adds a bolt to my studio door, afraid that even though the building I'm living in has a security guard, someone might try to rob or rape me.

When Nena came over, I thought she was coming to talk to me about Pepin. She has been worried about his marriage. His potential for violence toward his wife brought on by the stress of raising a small child is something she verbalizes to me often. Even though they haven't spoken to each other in more than a year, she has a constant worry about this situation. Pepin and Sandra have never spoken to me about any possible trouble in their marriage, and it is only through Nena that I am made aware of their troubles.

Now as I try to listen to what she is saying, I am mentally taking her to the local clinic. Awareness of HIV, now in the mid-eighties, is only beginning to emerge. A retrovirus that attacks a person's immune system, it is the secondary infections we are constantly treating since there is no medicine to eradicate the virus itself. This virus is claiming the lives of people in New York City, around the country, around the world while the medical community tries desperately to treat each opportunistic infection on a case-by-case basis, knowing that underlying the disorder is one agent attacking its victim's defense mechanisms.

But before I worry about Nena dying and the end of our human existence, I really want to pass this pharmacology exam, maybe even ace it. My mind starts to drift as I hear Nena cursing her man and his woman. I am thinking about the fact that I only have eighteen more hours to study for this exam. I will not sleep until after the exam. I will take advantage of every waking moment to memorize all neurotransmitters, their mechanism of action, and the anatomical parts of the body on which they exert their actions.

"Mom, let's go to the clinic to get you tested." I need to get this situation resolved quickly.

"No!" she yells back at me. "Haven't you been listening to me? Anyway, I'm healthy."

"Mom, the disease is not very well understood, but we now know that it's caused by a virus, and you can be healthy for a period of time before the virus begins to attack your immune system." I'm back to my all too familiar position of being rational and trying to decide upon a logical course of action. Resistance is what I'm met with.

"I came here to talk to you because you're my daughter, and you need to hear this stuff. If I want medical advice, I'll go to a real doctor," she says, puffing on her third cigarette. By now, I see that what she has really come to tell me is that she needs to be near someone who cares about her after her lover's betrayal. The fact that she may be infected with HIV and the worry that I now have about her status is not even something that occurred to her might be central to her view. I need some coffee.

"Mom, let's go to the diner across the street," I suggest.

"Oh, yes, I love diners." She continues her saga.

I have but one aim at this point in my life, and that is to become a doctor. I want to be able to heal in a manner that first impressed me as a teenager when I interacted with physicians when I took my grandmother to her doctors' appointments, and later as a candy striper volunteer. I saw in this profession humanism detached from emotions as doctors used their intellect to improve the state of health of our fellow man. That is, an involvement with others to make them better, without engaging in emotions. In fact, we are taught in medical school to maintain our objective distance from our patients as we compassionately use our medical knowledge to heal. (It was the field where my desire to make things right was augmented by my primary defense mechanism—detachment.)

My four years in college as a biology major were extremely challenging, and there were many difficult times where I thought I wasn't going to make it. But it was in overcoming this seemingly insurmountable obstacle where I found meaning and fulfillment. The angry energy I had inside was channeled toward the task of letting this chemistry class and that genetics lab and this calculus theorem know that they were not going to beat me. On campus, I met many like myself, people who looked forward to an intellectual challenge. Science is the field where we all come together in the wonderment of how our world works. My college life gave me this.

Now having successfully completed those four college years, and being granted my Cornell diploma, I am well on my way to becoming a doctor. I am living my dream.

As I listen to Nena before me now, I am trying to show I care about the details of this other woman's life and what a slut she is. However, what I really care about is having my mother tested for HIV. I want her to stop smoking, and I want to make sure violence doesn't follow from this piece of news.

I don't bring up the fact that I thought she wanted to visit to see how I was doing. Maybe she would make me *mangu con huevos* or some other delicious Dominican dish to help sustain me during exams. I still revert to my childhood notions that she will nurture me the way I see my classmates being looked after by their parents even though they are adults. I don't dare tell her now how I was stuck with the needle of an HIV-positive patient while learning how to draw blood and have so far tested negative for the antibody to the virus. I look at her and know such news would just cause her to scream hysterically and yell at me for not being careful.

I try to explain to her the importance of my exams and how hard I'm finding this topic I'm tackling at this moment, but she answers me, "*Libros, y libros, eso es todo lo que te importa, yo se que tu vas a sacar buenas notas, siempre lo haces, pero yo soy tu madre y me tienes que oír* [Books and books, that's all you care about, but I'm your mother, and you need to listen to me]." And so I do.

(Years from now when I'm doing my internship in Manhattan, she shows up at work unannounced, and I try to deal with her latest drama without letting any one of my colleagues get a hint of the social ills that plague my family. The racist comments against Dominicans are a daily barrage I try to ignore, but slowly they wear me down. One night while taking care of a premature infant, my senior resident, prominently displaying a religious symbol on him, states to me, "I just saved the life of a child who is going to grow up to mug my grandmother." He chuckles angrily at me. This newborn just a few hours old has been indicted.

And instead of comfort from my mother, I will try to ask her calmly to leave the hospital. "Mom, I'm doing a thirty-six-hour shift and have a lot of work to do. Please leave. I'll call you when I'm done." I try to shoo her away.

"*Mentira tuya* [That's a lie of yours]," she responds. "Everybody knows the body cannot resist all of those hours awake," she states, accusing me of not wanting to be with her.)

Before me right now, as she continues the details of how this virus is making its way through 176th Street, what I see before me is not just my mother, but a poor Hispanic patient, typical of the ones on whom we practice our interviewing skills. I can just hear my schoolmates snicker after she leaves. "Don't these people get it? Their irresponsible sexual behavior is what got this plague ravaging them, and here we have to treat them for something that could have been prevented if they'd only learn how to keep their pants zippered up."

I am so tired of talking to Nena, of trying to help her but always being met with resistance. She will not agree to be tested to see if she carries the HIV antibody. She doesn't want to hear my medical explanation for how to proceed in order to answer what most normal people would want to know—that is, is she positive? I feel my patience running out and the anger within me rising. However, I need to sit and listen.

After about two hours of nonstop talking, Nena is ready to leave. I walk her to the bus stop and let her know I'm worried about her health status. She promises to go to the doctor, and I allow my pity to show. "I'll come spend the night with you once my exams are over." I hug her.

She kisses me and says, "*Mi negra, te quierro.*"

Relieved to let her go, I call Nick so we can study together using his beautifully drawn notes. "Really, Nick, you should get all of your medical school notes published; this stuff is gold," I tell him, admiring his visual representations of our elusive descriptions of the chemicals that run through our body. More students come together, and we share our pieces of knowledge as we chew through pizzas, laugh with delirious exhaustion, and cram.

In the end, we all pass our exams!

The Strength to Change I

My two Cupie dolls have bathed, put their pajamas on, and read with me on our rocking chair, each on my lap, as we do every night. As I tuck them in on this Dr. Martin Luther King, Jr. Day, 2001, I say, "Three-day weekend, followed by a four-day school week. Which one is better?" "Three-day weekend, Mommy, of course," Sarah (my daughter, age ten) and Matthew (my son, age eight) answer, and we all laugh. I go off to bed exhausted, looking forward to a good night's sleep before I have to work tomorrow morning.

The phone rings. My husband answers, and he hears some voices speaking Spanish before they hang up on him. It's past ten o'clock at night. The phone rings again. "Mom?" I hear him ask. "Who is this . . . yes we'll be there right away." He hangs up. "Nell, that was your uncle Chano. Your brother Gilbert is dead."

I panic. My mind starts racing, but I don't want the children to know anything. I have kept them shielded from Gilbert's drug use, and now his tragic life is over, a life I will have to revisit with my children, but not tonight. I call a neighbor, who agrees to have her nanny sleep in my house. We speed to Washington Heights. On our way, I call Nena, but all I hear is confusion from her. "*Aaayyy, aaayyy, no se lo que paso . . . mi hijo!*" I hear her scream. Her friend Maria picks up the phone. "Nelita, *tu mama te necesita* [your mother needs you]," she says.

"I am almost there," I answer her in Spanish.

Nena is on her bed, surrounded by two of her brothers and their wives. She's holding onto Maria, and her eyes are wide open, looking disoriented and crying dry tears. Nena gives me brief eye contact and continues repeating "*Mi hijo, mi hijo.*" I go to the living room of the apartment we grew up in and see my brother's lifeless, purple body with a syringe still in his arm. On a small, foldable table are two large, empty cans of beer. My heart pumps so loudly it muffles my ability to hear. The shock of seeing his stiff corpse overwhelms me. I look around the living room for clues, not sure what I'm trying to piece together, when my eye falls on a religious symbol. Gilbert had pinned a cross on the collar of his jean jacket. This surprises me; I had never known him to be religious.

Gilbert was out of a rehabilitation center for the long weekend. Nena later told us how well he looked. He seemed happy, had gained weight, and was enthusiastically repeating his lessons learned about staying clean. He took Nena shopping to a mall in New Jersey earlier in the day, where he had an ear pierced. He bought Nena some clothes and repeated to her several times how, this time, he was really going to make it. Afterward, Gilbert went to a Martin Luther King ceremony where the words of his hero were an inspiration that he applied to himself and to his struggle with sobriety. When he got home, he went straight to the living room while Nena was cooking dinner. She asked him to come eat with her in the kitchen, but he responded, "Ma, I'll eat later. I'm really tired right now."

"Well, you'd better eat while the food is warm because I don't want to hear you making noise late at night heating up the food. Come eat while the food is warm," she repeated several times as she ate. Then it was time for the latest novella, and she took her food to her bedroom to watch *Betty La Fea*. During each commercial break, Nena yelled through the wall that separates the living room from the bedroom, "*Ve a comer.* I don't want you in that kitchen later." But she got no response. The novella was over. Nena got up and muttered to herself, "*Coño, ahora tengo que re-encalentar la comida* [Now I'm going to have to reheat the food]." She opened the living room door, repeating this same sentence over and over again. She saw Gilbert sitting on one of the chairs from her dinette set, head slumped back, syringe in his arm. This all-too-familiar scene of Gilbert strung out infuriated her. "How could he?" she asked herself. She pulled him up with his limp arms around her shoulders, and as she dragged him to lay him down on the sofa, they both fell onto the wooden floor. With his lifeless, purple face right up against hers, she started screaming. Nena's neighbors heard her piercing cry and ran over.

The apartment is now filling up with family and friends. Neida is especially distraught. When Nena left Gilbertico in the Dominican Republic, Neida took him in and always treated him as her son. "*Caminabamos siempre abrazado como dos novios. Tico, Tico, nooooooooo!*" she is howling in grief. Her son, my cousin Ochie, is also addicted to heroin. Right now he's in jail, where he has spent most of his adult life. It's the place about which Neida says, "I know he's safe." We all worry constantly about Ochie. Will he be the next to die like Gilbert?

Gilbert's only child, his daughter, Cindy, is inconsolable. The last time she saw her father was at her wedding. He refused to walk her down the aisle, they fought, and he spent the rest of that day hiding his tears.

Early the next morning, Gilbert is carried out in a body bag to another wave of screaming from Nena, Cindy, and the rest of the family. Neighbors come out of their apartments to watch the covered corpse being carried away. We run to the window to watch as Gilbert is placed into the medical examiner's van to the chorus of "*Ay, Gilbertico, nos dejate, ya se fue Gilbertico . . . Tico*[You left us, Gilbert)."

Nena kisses me and hugs me tightly. "Nelita, go home and take care of your children. I'm okay here with all of this company."

"Mami, I'll be back to make the funeral arrangements later, *tranquila,*" I answer. As we ride back to my home in Scarsdale, I remember one of the last times I saw Gilbert. It was New Year's Day. Nena had stayed over to share the countdown with me on December 31, 2000, so I had to drive her home the next day. Gilbert was hanging out on the corner when he saw my car and came over. He was wearing a camel-hair coat, silk scarf neatly tucked in the breast pocket, and fashionable sunglasses. He put his head in through the driver's side window and kissed me. "I'm still partying, Nell. This is going to be a good year." He was smiling, missing his front tooth, and pulled a bottle of Tanqueray from inside his coat. "What? It's New Year's" was his response to my disapproving look. He reached over and kissed me several times more. "You know, you don't know what it's like living with this woman and that mouth of hers," he said, referring to Nena, laughing while he drank straight from the bottle. It was a cold, grey day, and I felt my throat clamping as I was about to cry.

"Gil, how's Cindy?" I asked about his daughter.

"Beautiful. That girl is the best. You should see how well behaved she is, and she's so smart! She's doing really well in school. I want her to be just like you. I keep telling her I want her to be just like my sister. Will you help her?" He was in a good mood, laughing in between swigs of his liquor. I was becoming depressed, wondering what drug cocktail he was on.

"Of course, I'll help her in any way I can." And now I had to make my exit. I normally would have stopped and let him ramble on about how he was "gonna make it" and allow him to air his dreams we both knew would never come true. At this moment, however, I was about to cry at the sight of him, a well-known addict in my old neighborhood, notorious for his temper and wild escapades. During his teenage years, he had been arrested for throwing bricks at cars driving onto the entrance ramp of the George Washington Bridge. I never knew if anyone was hurt as a result, but these delinquent acts earned him his street name, "Luquillo," meaning "the crazy one."

I found my way out of listening to him going on lecturing. "Gilbert, give my love to Cindy. I need to get home to my kids."

"Bye, Nells." This time, he kissed and then pinched my cheeks.

I drove toward the Cross Bronx Expressway, and as I passed Public School 115, I saw sheets of metal covering the entrance to its courtyard. I remembered once standing in this courtyard with my grandmother, Mama, waiting for Ochie after school. Mama, another well-known figure in our neighborhood, nicknamed "Cantinflas" because of her humor, tripped on a piece of metal and fell flat on her face. A group of young kids nearby started laughing at her. I was shaking with fear when I helped her off the ground. She dusted herself off, laughing after her initial scream. I must have trembled for at least an hour after seeing her fall. I was maybe seven or eight years old and almost her size. I put my arm around her waist and would not let her go, feeling the frailty of her bones. At the moment she fell over, I thought she could have died. This courtyard was where we played for hours as children: kickball, stickball, handball, red-light-green-light, one-two-three, and of course, dodge ball. I now faced this empty courtyard, with sheets of metal swaying in the wind, blocking its entrance. At the sight of this horrendously ugly attempt to limit children from playing in a perfectly useable space, my tears spilled over. Why would anyone conceal a playground this way? That day, I drove up and down the Bronx River Parkway, waiting for my tears to abate before going home to my husband and children. I did not want to start the new year with the cloud of my disturbed family hanging over us.

My poor brother is dead, and we arrive at our house. No time for sleep because I have to get my children ready for school. I will tell them tonight that their uncle Gilbert is dead because of his abuse of drugs and alcohol. Our morning routine completed, I drop Sarah and Matthew off at school. Now it's time for me to start making phone calls. I call Pepin, whom I know is probably at his job, and when he answers, I say, "Peps, Gilbert is dead."

"About time the nigger died" is his answer.

"When can you get up here?" I ask, assuming he will not miss the funeral and ignoring his cruel comment.

"I'm not spending a dime on that mother-fucker. One less piece of shit for society to deal with." His answer both saddens and angers me. Pepin becomes different people at different times; the voice of this one disgusts me. I fear every day for the anger within Pepin that has deepened now with his job as a corrections officer.

"You mean you're not going to be here for your mother during this time?" I ask, incredulous.

"Just because she fucked Gil's father don't make him my brother. You don't know all the things he did, Nell, because you were always buried in your books. I was raised on the streets and saw things you don't even have a clue about. Yeah, I have to admit, he did defend me sometimes against some thugs, but some of the shit he did, Nell, I never told you. It was just too ugly. I had to leave Washington Heights in 1989 because I was going to kill one of those Dominican crackheads. It was a war, and Gilbert was on the enemy's side. Dominican drug dealers took over the neighborhood and had us all terrorized. You just don't know—"

"Don't tell me! I don't know!" I shout back. "Every day I went to work in Washington Heights and had to hear my colleagues make horrible comments about the Dominicans there. One day I attended the delivery of a premature baby born to a Dominican woman, and my senior resident said, 'I just saved the life of a kid who is going to grow up and mug my grandmother.' He made this comment to hurt me, knowing I was from the neighborhood. But I didn't respond. These racist and cruel statements almost paralyzed me. Knowing Gilbert was just a few blocks away, selling junk at the 178th Street bus terminal, is one reason I never spoke up about this harassment I dealt with, as if I were the guilty party. So don't tell me I don't know. Those starving children we saw on our trip to the Dominican Republic are some of the ones selling crack because it's better than dying of hunger."

Pepin interrupts me. "Cut the liberal crap and let me tell you something about your brother, the junkie. I never wanted you to know this, but I want to give you an example of what that piece of shit you call a human being used to do. Remember that time he showed up at the Columbia-Presbyterian emergency room full of stab wounds?"

"Of course, I remember; he had been mugged in the Bronx and, despite all of his wounds, managed to drive himself to Washington Heights—"

Pepin cut me off. "He was stabbed in the Bronx, but it wasn't a mugging. A pimp got a hold of Gilbert and stabbed him about eight times in retaliation."

"In retaliation for what?" I'm shocked, and my head is swirling with so many emotions. "To get money for drugs, Gil would go under the Bruckner Expressway, pick up hookers, and beat them up for their cash. He liked seeing them all bruised up and stumbling away from him. He'd laugh as he told the story around the block, bragging about what he'd done. That nigger got what he had coming, should've died back then when they took out half his liver. Several times Gilbert had a hit out on him. A lot of people wanted him dead over the years. One of them was a numbers runner whose kid Gil got addicted to heroin. And now you're calling me to tell me to come up for his funeral? Nell, take my advice, take care of your kiddies, take care of yourself, and forget about the latest drama in Mom's life."

"Pepin, I have to go, I'm exhausted, I haven't slept, and I have so much to do."

"Nelly, I love you. Please don't let these people suck you in. Give your kiddies a hug and kiss from their uncle Joe."

"I have to keep going," I say to myself, because my reality is that I cannot break down. It is a luxury that for me will never be indulged. There is no one to whom I can fully unload all of this burden; there never has been anyone. Nelita, that one who is always there to comfort, counsel, help with bail money, help with back-rent money, listen and try to referee the latest fight Nena has had. And now I'm the one that has to arrange this funeral, including paying for it. While I have been described by Pepin as being made of rock, and he has said, usually while crying about our childhood, "You don't seem to feel emotions, things the way I feel them," he is wrong. I just don't allow my emotions to control my life. I am also not stuck in the past. I read somewhere that objects of worship are made out of stone, because we can lay our problems onto them, because they are unbreakable. But at moments such as this one, knowing that I need my brother Pepin, and instead, he responds so cruelly, my loneliness starts to overwhelm me. I want nothing more at times like these than to lie in bed, crying and sleeping, but I cannot allow myself such an indulgence. And in my mind, I excuse Pepin for the way he has responded in this time of crisis. He has become the type of angry, tense man that makes me wonder if he will snap at any moment. All the more reason I need to try to ease each storm as it occurs in Nena's life. Nelita, detached, calm, reliable, always there when needed, is my role in this family. Besides, I have my children to think about. My entire life, I have tried to be as different from Nena as possible, and displaying dramatic emotions like she would is something I swore I would never do in front of my children. As a pediatrician, I've learned about the harmful effects depression and mood disorders in the mother, can have on their children. So I hold it all in. Despite the harm it does to me emotionally, I cannot walk away from my family when they need me.

The Strength to Change II

Gilbert on Angel's lap on left
Pepin and Nelita sitting upper right

Nelita, Pepin and Gilbertico 1965

Nena is sitting on her bed, going through papers and ripping some up. I slept over to keep her company after Gilbertico's funeral. Our neighbors, as always, have been there for us. They have packed Nena's refrigerator with food, *salcocho, arroz con pollo, pastelitos de carne*, and several pitchers of *morir sonando*. Packets of Huberplex, a tranquilizer, are stacked on Nena's night table next to her cigarettes, powdered foundation makeup, and tangy colored lipstick. Her neighbor Lourdes even made a black suit for Nena to wear today, all in one night. I look closely and notice that the loose leaf papers she is tearing into small squares are handwritten notes. I ask, "What is this?"

"*Porquería que Gilbertico escribía cuando estaba en su asunto de curarse* [Garbage Gilbert wrote while trying to cure himself in rehab]," she tells me. "I want to read them." I grab the few pages left that are intact. It's his voice. The writing is candid, straight from the heart, full of feelings I thought he was no longer capable of experiencing since he was numbing himself. He truly wanted to recover from his multiple addictions, and the pain of this struggle is palpable as his words find their way to me. Nena just sits by my side, surprising me with her calm. I thought these letters and my wanting to read them would cause a fight between us. Gilbert had remorse for the women he mistreated and named one whom he regretted beating. He recounted one episode when she greeted him in their apartment wearing an elaborate white lace nightgown. She prepared his favorite dishes for a romantic dinner. Instead of enjoying the romantic evening she had planned for them, he unleashed his rage on her by sending the food flying around the kitchen and beating her. Then he tried to choke her as he insulted the small town of Navarette in the Dominican Republic she was from. He ended the evening by locking her in a closet and leaving the apartment. "I just cannot explain what would come over me," he wrote. "I feel so GUILTY; this woman was just there to cook for me, she wanted to take care of me, but seeing her act like a hick angered me for no reason. That explosion came out of nowhere, I just wanted to beat her . . . WHY? I don't know what comes over me when I lose it like that." I am struck by his capitalizing the word "guilty," a word he capitalized again in reference to giving some of his girlfriends gonorrhea. As he looked back on these cruel deeds while in recovery, he did feel the heaviness of making others suffer while he was high. In these words, I see a new side of him. Many people had given up on him. I too stopped believing he wanted to stop getting high. I yearned for a sober brother who lived a "normal" life so that I could share more positive moments with him. I also believe "it isn't over until it's over" and that people could beat this terrible disease of addiction.

Now that I realize he felt guilt and had remorse, I understand a pattern with him. Why would he continuously fall back into his drug and alcohol habit? Could it be that while sober, the crushing guilt led him to start getting high again? That while sober he could not face all the destruction he created while high? This feeling I think was part of his inability to stay sober. His guilt along with his intense physical cravings made me think again of a medical fact regarding psychiatric conditions, both nature and nurture contributing to these conditions. "In heroin, I found the warmth I craved from my mother," wrote Gilbert, expressing the rejection he felt from Nena. I am also struck by how much he sounds like Pepin when referring to Nena. Both had such a tortuous relationship with her. Gilbert's being left behind in the Dominican Republic was an act he took to mean his mother did not want him. When he came to the United States and found that Nena had a new family, a "white" family, it confirmed his feelings of being unwanted. But he came to love Angel Maseda. He wrote, "If Mom and Angel would have stayed together, my life would've turned out very different. I loved that man. Every time he saw me, he gave me a hug and a kiss and would have me sit on his lap while he told me about the musicians and explained to me the different instruments *soneros* use. He was the coolest dude I ever knew."

I never realized Angel's leaving us also destroyed Nena's other boy. Another letter opens up with, "I loved my job with Con Edison. I could've stayed there forever. For the first time in my life, I looked forward to getting up and going to work. I never missed a day in my six years there. Then Nancy Reagan went around the country talking about 'just say no to drugs' in the 1980s. Just say no? What is she saying? This thing is not like that. You just can't put the junk down and stop all of a sudden. But I'm trying. The methadone helps me, and I get high a lot less. It helps me do my job. Then they started random drug testing at work, and I'm fucked! I lost my job and god-damit, I could do my job while on methadone maintenance, but the zero tolerance hit the country. 'Just say no' is not that easy when you're at the stage of addiction where you need the stuff just to keep yourself from getting sick!"

As I read this confession, I learn something new about him again. In this new millennium, the correct use of methadone might have allowed him to keep his job, as long as his performance was judged to be unhampered by this medical intervention. I see another possibility that would have made a difference in Gilbert's life. After being fired, he found himself in a decline back into the world of drug dealing, excessive heroin use, and daily alcohol drinking as well as using other illegal substances.

My brother Gilbertico spent so much time in self-loathing. I wish I could have told him so much. The fact is, he was my hero when he put an end to Nena's bringing home perverts. Gilbert, you were one of my protectors in life. Everyone in the neighborhood knew you didn't mess with Luquillo's little sister.

"Cindy, I have letters your father wrote while in rehab that I want you to have," I tell Gilbert's grieving daughter.

"Nelita, I already read some I found in Abuela's apartment. Nelita, I never knew he was a heroin addict. I knew about the alcohol, but not the heroin. Why didn't anybody tell me?" she asks.

"Cindy, the whole neighborhood knew!" I am incredulous.

"Nelita, I read in one of the letters that when his father, Pirulo, used to torture people in the Dominican Republic, he sometimes made my father watch. My dad wrote about watching his father beat and rape women. He was really devastated when his mother left for the United States and hated being with his father. After he went to live with Neida and Mama, he wrote about how he loved sleeping in between them in one bed. When Pirulo came to pick him up, he ran and hid because he was afraid of his father. What do you know about this? When he returned to Santo Domingo after Nena's divorce from Angel, he says you guys all ignored him and left him behind again. But about my grandfather, Nelly, what do you know?" she asks me.

I had read in some Dominican history books that Gilberto Sanchez Rubirosa, Pirulo, had access to several houses dedicated to the torture of political dissidents under Trujillo. It has been written that these tormentors stuck pins into people's eyes, electrocuted their testicles, and after inflicting inconceivable torture on others, made the bodies disappear. "About anything specific Pirulo did, I only know that he was a very evil man and had to go live in Spain under political asylum after Trujillo was killed. Nena doesn't talk about that part of her life, so I know very little about this stage. Cindy, when I ask your *abuela* about that period in her life, she always answers, '*Eso se borro*,' that is erased." I also realize as I say this that I too have many more questions about this man, about Nena's relationship with Pirulo, about her life in general in the Dominican Republic, that I'll never know the answers to. "Cindy, you were the light of his life. He adored you. Unfortunately, Gilbert pursued heroin, rather than pay more attention to you, because he was a slave to his addiction. He was very affectionate toward you, and I want you to remember those moments with your father. You made Gilbert very happy, probably the only person who made him feel the joy of pure love." I try to console her sobs.

Weeks later, when I go to collect these letters for Cindy to keep as a piece of her father she can claim, the letters are gone. Nena made sure no trace of them remained. "*Una vida entera* [An entire lifetime] looking for him in alleyways after not hearing from him for days, middle of the night phone calls to come pick him up in some whore's house because he couldn't move. *Luche, y luche y luche ese maldito muchacho me dio tanto trabajo desde que nacio* [I struggled, he gave me trouble since the day he was born]." Nena is screaming these words and crying at the same time.

"And now it's over, Mommy. Finally he's in peace," I try to console her as I gently fix her hair and wipe away the tears from her face. It is the only reason I can think of for why she would tear up Gilbert's words. It's finally over.

Pepin's Fortieth Birthday

Christina, Pepin and Sandra on August 1, 2001

"Nells, look—the same face," Pepin says to me, pointing to a picture of Angel and me. He then squeezes my cheeks, calls me Cuqui (one of our invented words), and kisses them. I came down to Miami from New York with Nena to spend Pepin's fortieth birthday with him today, August 1, 2001. He has been working as a federal corrections officer for years in a job that he seems to be doing well in. Living with his wife, Sandra, and daughter, Christina, in a beautiful three-bedroom home with a nice backyard and pool—that is his pride. Always being able to fix anything from blenders, to car engines, even connecting many people to illegal cable television at the age of eleven, Pepin has always been a wiz at being able to rehabilitate items, as is evident in this home. The ceramic tiling that covers the entire house rarely has chipped off pieces because Pepin measured and remeasured and remeasured the floor to minimize each room's areas of asymmetry in the size of each tile. "Damn, that little triangle here drives me crazy," he says of a piece where he had no choice but to cut into odd shapes and therefore throw off his schematics.

"Peps, you can't even notice it," I tell him. But I've already seen after a few hours here how much worse his obsessive compulsive disorder has become. The different remote controls have to point in a certain direction, he has already done his daily bacterial count of the pool and made adjustments accordingly, and he times people taking a shower and knocks on the door to let the person know the hot water tank is about to run out. He showed me binders he keeps in his garage detailing every aspect of car maintenance for each of the three automobiles in the home. The mileage on each timing belt, the date of the last oil change he performed, the condition of each spark plug on such and such a date. He has even calculated what is more cost effective for their commutes—that is, whether the extra distance to avoid a certain toll justifies the money spent on gas for the extra miles on the side streets. The worst part of his endless obsessions is how these compulsions affect him. Like a person standing on unsteady ground that might at any moment collapse, he never seems comfortable, has not a moment to relax.

For those of us in his presence, the tension is like walking on eggshells; you never know what you might do wrong that will set him off. Despite the open affection that Pepin sincerely showers on Christina and Sandra, I can't help but feel sorry for them living under this constant pressure. Everything bothers him, and at times it seems like barking orders, such as "Don't touch that! Careful where you put that glass of water" and on and on and on, are all you hear from his extremely tense self. This worries me, wondering when his volcano of anger will explode. I try to soothe him as we look through this album I made for him as a birthday present. I have put a chronology of pictures of him from infancy to the present. We are past pictures with Pops now, where Pepin momentarily teared up and thought his depression would end our present contentment of being together. Now he is laughing at his disco stage. "I can't believe

I fit into those Sergio Valente jeans! A fart couldn't squeeze through those butt cheeks with them pants on," he says, cracking up.

"Yeah, I used to have to lie down on the bed just to get the zipper up! We wanted them so tight," I say, laughing. We go over that time in our lives when I left for college, and Pepin stayed behind with Gilbert and Nena in our apartment. My two brothers had dropped out of high school, and what I was told, years later, is that there was constant fighting between those three in that one-bedroom apartment. Pepin eventually moved out into a rented room while he worked as a janitor. A job description that broke Nena's heart every time she spoke of it. "My son, the smartest of my three kids, working at a job with illegal immigrants" was one of her laments. A job he kept after Sandra became pregnant with Christina, a job he rose to a management position in. He had to eventually leave it due to constant fighting with coworkers and subordinates. As I rest my head on his muscular, hairy chest, his strong arms around me, I hug him and think of how much I miss him, how much I wish he could put to rest his demons. Neither Pepin, Sandra, nor their teenage daughter, Christina, has ever confirmed this for me, but Nena told me that Pepin has been beating on Sandra regularly since the time she became pregnant. It sickens me to think of this. I've been told of the many times that safe passage for Sandra has been offered for her to leave her abusive husband, but she defends him and claims to love him. In fact, a few years ago, I happened to find out that Christina was living in Ecuador, a move I was not informed of. This was the result of a beating Pepin gave to one of Christina's boyfriends who then threatened to bring charges. Social services investigated the family, and by making Christina leave the country, the matter was dropped. Years after this incident, I found out from Nena why Christina was sent away.

Watching Sandra and Pepin kiss and hug several times today, it is hard to imagine this dark side of their relationship. I see that beautiful, little boy that shared a twin bed with me transformed into a very sad, angry, pumped up, steroid-looking hulk. "Pepin, you look like you've been using steroids, and the side effects are . . .

even psychosis," I say to him. He never denies using this dangerous substance to increase his muscle mass, a practice known to be very common among corrections officers, but he never admits it either.

"Look at this, Nelly. Your brother still sleeps on the same pillow he used as a little boy!" Sandra laughs, showing me the flattened pillow with yellow stains and layers of lint. He brought back this pillow from Puerto Rico in 1974.

"I can't sleep without my pillow. Shit, I fold that thing over ten times, put my head on it, and I'm out. Ain't no pillow in the world, I don't care how much it costs, could replace this old thing," he says. Then he jumps over to where Nena put her coffee cup down. "Damn, Mom, you just don't put your *taza* down anywhere, *por lo menos*, put a napkin under it." "*Mi hijo.*" Nena wraps her arms around his waist. "*Por favor tranquilízate.* I want to see you calm for once in my life," she says and then repeats that she cannot believe her little ball of swiss cheese is now forty. "That's what your father used to say you looked like when we brought you home from the intensive care unit as a baby, '*una bola de quezo.*'" We become self-conscious that when Angel Maseda is mentioned, it can trigger Pepin's tears of sadness.

A portrait of our father hangs on the living room wall. Occasionally, Peps looks at it and says, "My old man, the only person who truly loved me." As he stares at this picture of a handsome Angel Maseda, greased back hair and cigarette in his hand, I have learned never to utter a single negative word against our father. Once during one of our long phone calls where Pepin went on and on recounting ways in which Nena humiliated him, I stated that part of the blame for our circumstances as children lay on Angel Maseda. I reminded Pepin that it was he who left, who abandoned us and left us to be raised by a woman who could not handle the awesome responsibility of parenting us. I said this in an effort to have Pepin gain some empathy for Nena. Instead, he went on a tirade, one of the very few times he yelled at me during these phone calls. "Don't you dare ever say anything against my old man!" he screamed. When he called me back a few days later, he said in his depressed, barely audible whisper, "It's that, Nell, if I believe that man did not love me, I would have to kill myself."

Christina, sensing she cannot let her father sink into sadness at this moment, states, "Time to cut the cake." I point my video camera at Pepin and ask him to say something. He cups his hand over his mouth, points to Nena, and says into the camera, "I wish I never had you," referring to our mother's almost daily rant when we were children. Nena did not hear this.

"Mom, say something to the camera about your baby boy turning forty."

"As a single mother, I gave my children all they needed . . ."

Pepin stands behind Nena, making faces at her while Sandra and Christina laugh.

Pressure Phone Calls

Pepin The Federal Corrections Officer

The children are in bed, and I'm now falling asleep when the phone rings.

"Hi, Nell." It's Pepin in a low voice.

"Is everything okay?" I ask in a startled voice.

"I was sitting watching television, and a memory came to me that has filled me with so much rage, I just want to go to New York and stick a knife in our mother's neck."

"Pepin, tell me what's going on. It's ok, calm down, tell me what's happening."

"Nell, right now my blood is boiling, and my heart is beating so fast I think I'm having a panic attack." His voice is still low, but the volume is increasing along with his agitation.

"If you want to tell me about your memory, go ahead, I'm listening. Tell me everything you are feeling." I try to calm down and revert to a soothing voice.

"I remember waking up in the middle of the night—we were very young, maybe six and seven—and I felt like I needed to pee. But then I heard some other sounds as I walked to the bathroom, and then I saw it." He stops for a long pause. "She was fucking two black guys at the same time. I just stood there and stared. Now, Nelly, when I think about this, all I want to do is harm her. How could she do this to us?" he says, his voice rising.

"She did things that no mother should have had her children watch, but who were these guys? How come I don't remember this?" Now I'm injecting myself into the memory.

"She had given us sleeping pills, which always knocked you out, but those things hardly touched me."

"Yes, I remember once a sleeping pill she gave me that knocked me out for an entire weekend." My memory of being given these pills was actually a tender one, my mother always patient and loving when she gave them to us, as if every mother in America were lovingly drugging their children to sleep as an act of love.

"It was those two black guys—a tall, mute one who communicated in sign language and the short one with glasses. If they were in front of me right now, I would stick my boot down their throat, those motherfuckers," he says, his vengeance fantasies now becoming clear.

"You mean the guys who built the shelves in the living room?" I remembered when they drilled the metal brackets into the wall and mounted the wooden shelves. It made our living room seem cool, modern. We put our stereo system on one level and the encyclopedia

Britannica, which we had been given by a neighbor who was moving out, on another level.

"Yeah, why do you think they built those shelves for her? I swear to God, Nelly, I have so much rage right now I can hardly think. I just want to kill her—all that she did, those perverts she let in the house, why doesn't she just die? Maybe if she died, I'd have some peace." I can tell he's crying now. "You know that Frank Sinatra song 'Strangers in the Night'? I can't even listen to it. Whenever I hear it somewhere, I just get sick to my stomach. She was always singing that song, and I could just picture that bitch-whore smiling to herself thinking about the fucking she had done and the more fucking she was going to do with those assholes."

I have to proceed very carefully when he is in this state. Anything I say at moments like these can make the difference between an act of violence of his toward an innocent bystander or his coming down from this rage. Since my mother made me aware that there was domestic violence in his relationship with his wife, I now realize that at moments such as this when his anger makes him act without allowing time for his intellect to control his actions, whoever is near him can get hurt. I have also been told by my cousins who live in Miami that there are numerous complaints against Pepin for excessive use of force against the inmates he guards. Pepin thinks I don't know any of this. Holding the phone at this moment, what I feel most of all is fear. Is he holding a gun to his head? Has he just beaten his wife? What has he done at work as a result of unleashing this enormous rage he carries? A rage sometimes tamed when he crashes into depression. The last time I saw him with those pumped up arms, I just knew he was using steroids. As a medical professional, we are trained to pick up these physical signs. What does he do when his violent tendencies are intermixed with the steroid-induced psychosis? More for me to worry about.

So much tension when I allow myself to feel my brother's rage, such a feeling of helplessness when you cannot intervene to protect others from a mentally ill person unless you have firsthand knowledge of an act against others that they've committed, and even then, it is the victim who must press charges. There is nothing I can do unless I have proof that there is imminent danger to himself or others.

I think to myself sometimes, how long have I felt this enormous tension of my brother's episodic fantasies of hurting my mother? I remember when I was in first grade, I had a very vivid dream that, thirty-five years later, I still sometimes think about. In the dream, Pepin was dressed in a cowboy outfit, complete with a holster belt. He shoots his gun and blows on the smoke that comes out of the pistol, but it isn't a toy pistol as it should be if being handled by a seven-year-old boy. The pistol has shot a real bullet, and with it, he killed our mother. I woke up with a panic, looked around, and tightly held Nena, with whom I was sharing our twin bed. I looked over, and Pepin was sound asleep in his bed. It has been said that there are some truths revealed to us in dreams. This was one of them.

It is not only at this moment as I hold the telephone receiver against me with panic and pain, proceeding gently against the hurricane brewing inside of my brother. It isn't only at this moment that I fear for what he is capable of doing, from committing a mass shooting to humiliating women to self-murder. It is always simmering within me, this fear. I live with it—whether in my conscious awareness, as at this moment, or when I push it out of my mind and continue with my daily activities of tending to my family, my work. It's always there, the worry, the fear, the panic.

"Have you seen a professional in mental health? Pepin, you have got to seek help with a psychiatrist to put these past events to rest, to make peace with your mother, to stop reenacting the rage fantasies you feel for all the wrong that was done to you." I have been pleading with him for years to receive psychiatric treatment. "I started seeing someone when Matthew was three and Sarah five. At that age, I found myself constantly yelling at them, and although I know it may not sound unusual, I feared I might become Mom. The therapy sessions helped me get this anger out, Pepin. We carry so much of it that I fear it's poisoning us." I hope being open about my seeking help with a mental health professional helps him see there is no shame in it.

"Those perverts . . . and then I'd go to school smelling like urine, and the other kids would make fun of me and run away from me . . . why did Pops have to die? He was the only one who loved me." Pepin is sobbing now, and we have to revisit together those moments of rejection, those moments where we knew we were unwanted children. "Why was I born? I never should've been born. I came to this fucking world for nothing, just to suffer."

"You came to save my life. That time in Isla Verde Beach when I was drowning, you didn't think twice to jump in and save me from the undertow as it was taking me out into the middle of the ocean," I say to him soothingly, reminding him of all the good he is capable of. "You jumped in—" I say, and then he interrupts me.

"Yeah, I picked you up and kept throwing you toward the shore like Superman. We'd get thrown away from the shoreline, and I had to pick you up and throw you as far as I could until I got your ass to the shore. Nell, it was so easy; you were like a feather." His voice is becoming a little more animated.

"You were always trying to imitate Superman or any of those superhero comics. Remember the time you started a fire in Leda's kitchen, and then you ran to the bathroom, tied a towel around your neck, ran back to the trash can where the flames were now hitting the ceiling, and started blowing on the fire, thinking you could extinguish a fire by blowing on it like Superman? I panicked, ran to Leda, Gabriella, and some other people who were sitting in the living room. They screamed and then formed a line, passing down pots of water to throw on the fire. You were so cute, my little superhero." My love for that little boy is so strong, as I remember the beautiful boy with blond hair and the carefully tied knots from the towel around his neck. I am enveloped by the love we share. It was as if he and I were inside of an eggshell together, protecting our childhoods by creating our own happiness against the outside world.

"I bet Mom was out looking for Mr. Goodbar while this shit was going down—fucking whore. You know, Nell, what they should do with mothers like ours? Line them all up and shoot them, one by one. Let's get rid of the scum once and for all." I hated it when he spoke this way. Yet I had to let him share what was really going on inside. He could become another person, not the victim on the phone right now. He becomes the one in control, the one with power, the callous victimizer.

So many times, I wanted to share some of my most painful memories with him to heal myself, to tell him what I remember, especially about the sexual abuse, but I couldn't. He could snap at any moment, and rather than relive these evil moments of our past with all of its charged feelings, I needed to pull him out of it at moments like these. I needed to remind him of all that was good within him.

I cannot bring this up with the one person in the world who knows my deepest pain. The few times I have tried to talk about these incidents in my naïve attempts to heal him, instead what is unleashed is the monster he sometimes turns into.

Sometimes it was me who would call him when Nena got me so angry I thought I might want to slap her. Only Pepin could understand me at those moments. Like the time I took her out on Easter with my two children, Sarah two years old and my son an infant. We met our neighbors Ada, Nellie, and Migdalia Archilla at Saint Patrick's Cathedral, all dressed in Easter pastels. After walking around Rockefeller Center, we went to eat at a restaurant. The two generations divided into our respective conversations, Nena and Ada catching up and reviewing their favorite activity, gambling. Nellie, Migdalia, and I began talking about the death of the Tejana star Selena. Nena overheard me say what was a common thought at the time, that "Selena is more famous now in death than she was in life."

Nena looked over to me with a look as if I had done something terribly wrong and said "*Que dijiste?* Did you just say what I think you said? That Selena is more famous now in death than she was in life? Who the hell do you think you are? The daughter of blond, blue-eyed Gringos?"

I tell Peps, recounting this story, how the day turned from peaceful enjoyment of celebrating this holiday with my mother and my children, enjoying the hugs and kisses of their grandmother, to another ruined attempt at normalcy on my part. What did I say now to set her off? "Peps, what gets into her? She got up from her chair as her voice got louder. Others in the restaurant stopped their conversations to turn and look at us because here she was again, creating a scene. My two babies having to witness this, and the poor Archillas, who are so kind and jovial, will just sit there and take this outburst."

"The Washington Heights Rodriguez at it again," says Pepin.

"*Solo una arrepentida puede decir eso.* You, who are ashamed to be Latina, would say that of one of our great role models. If *you* did not know who Selena was, it is because you have chosen to forget your *Hispanidad* as you live your life as an educated doctor. But let me tell you, *muchachita*, the blood that runs through your veins is not *Gringa*," Nena said, tracing a line up her arm with her finger, her voice now explosive.

"Mom, can you name one single song of Selena's?" I ask her, knowing that she was not familiar with Selena's body of work, especially the hit "I'm Dreaming of you Tonight."

"Peps, that was like throwing gasoline into the fire, the fact that she could not answer my question. That woman grabbed her purse, and as she walked out of the restaurant, she shook her finger at me, accusing me of forgetting my roots and telling me how she is not going to even call me for 'a long time.'" I am now very emotional as I tell Pepin this. "Thank God our friends were there to remind me that it's just another Nena drama scene."

"Nelita, I don't know how you survived your mother. You know she has a problem. We were always praying for you," Ada said to me as she held my hand under the table.

"But it was that mouth that got the super up on Sunday mornings in the winter to turn the boiler on so we could have some heat in our building. That scary mouth of hers that I sometimes hated did get stuff done," Migdalia says. They are all trying to comfort me as I hug my children in an effort to counter the Nena effect.

"Nells, Mom is a loony. I don't understand how an educated person like you, a doctor no less, lets that loony bin get to you.

Dolly is right about that superintendent of our building, Rigo, fuckin' wife beater. Remember, Nell, how he would take his wife out in her underwear and beat her in the courtyard while we all watched? It went on until someone, usually Benny from the first floor, would smack him down. And to think that scum bag who hits women was afraid of Mom," he says chuckling.

A few days later on New Year's Eve, 2003, we're on the phone for hours. "Nelly, I barricaded the house, shut the windows with nails, and loaded the guns. I think Sandra is coming back to kill me. That bitch is crazy." He's in one of his states, and now I'm frozen with fear. How do I proceed?

"Pepin, unload the guns. What if Christina walks in, and you accidentally shoot her? What is happening? Tell me everything." I am both angry and petrified. Years of his going into states of irrational behavior, and no one does anything. Despite numerous visits by the police to this home, his wife will downplay these incidents and give me her classic explanation. "Oh, Nelly, you just have to ignore him. These moments just pass" is Sandra's patented answer. Tonight, I'm calling the police. "Peps, enough. Check yourself into a hospital for a mental rest. You need serious psychiatric treatment, and a scenario like you're describing right now is proof of your paranoid thinking."

"Careful what you say. I think the phones might be bugged."

"By whom?" I say as I realize how far gone he is.

"By the government. Working in the federal prisons, there's a lot of things I know they wouldn't want me telling anyone . . . Nell, Sandra hit herself and then went around to her friends saying I did it. She went crazy on me, and now I think she's going to kill me." He goes on to describe the details involved in hammering nails into the window frames carefully enough so as not to destroy the integrity of the wood. He fears for his life but still pays attention to the details of not ruining a coat of paint while reinforcing his home against an imminent attack.

"If what you are saying is true, either you call the police, or I'm going to call them, and if I call them from New York, they may not follow up because I am not directly involved. Do you want to do that to me on New Year's Eve?" I'm really getting agitated, which is one of the worst things he can hear in my voice. He calls the police, and while we await their arrival, he agrees something has been very wrong with him for a very long time—which he blames Nena for. Nevertheless, it's time to stop reliving what cannot be changed and to get treatment to stop the madness.

The police arrive. I am on the phone listening to the conversation until the cops ask him to get off the phone. I ring in New Year's with my children and our guests whom I've ignored for hours. My friend comforts me. She knows about the years of these types of phone calls from my brother, and the man just will not go for help. It has really taken a toll on me. Trying to keep my children unaware of this disturbance is my priority, but I'm sometimes torn between my daily life as a physician, mother, and wife and my need to "save" Pepin and thereby risk getting swallowed up in his insanity, as is happening during this night of supposed festivity. My anger and frustration grows larger since I am powerless to convince Pepin to check himself into a psychiatric hospital, or to at least stick with treatment. Furthermore, the only people who can go through the steps of forcing treatment upon Pepin are Pepin himself or one of his victims as a result of pressing charges, something his wife, Sandra, is never willing to do.

The New Year is here. I have hope. In 2004, Pepin will finally enter into acceptance of how serious his condition is, and we can finally restore what I have longed for, a healthy relationship with the brother whom I adore.

I call him back. "Nell, I couldn't do it . . . I'll lose my job if I end up in the psychiatric emergency room . . . I told the cops my wife hit me and that I was concerned she would be back to kill me. They took the report and left. You have to understand, I'll get fired and lose everything if it's on my record I'm seeing a psychiatrist." It's a speech I've heard many times before, given by both him and his wife.

A few days later, I call Pepin on his cell phone, and Sandra answers. "Sandra, it's Nelita. How are you? What's going on over there?" I ask.

"Oh, Jose had one of his episodes, and I went to my friend's house for New Year's until he got over it. Everything is fine, you know how he is . . ." Her usual speech.

Pepin gets on the phone. "Nell, I have to fight for my family." This is his explanation for why they are back together.

"You're now fighting for the family you were barricading yourself against just a few days ago?" I am so angry and disgusted; these roller-coaster rides are draining. "Well, are we going to Santo Domingo in February like we planned? You need to relax and maybe think about taking a leave of absence from work so you can spend a few months with our cousin Eufres on the island. You know you need it! If you won't start seeing a psychiatrist here, then some time away might help." I'm starting to yell.

"Nell, now is not the right time. I have to work on keeping my family together. I'm sorry I have to cancel this trip. You know I love you, Nell."

"I love you too, Peps." I hang up the phone, not knowing what to feel.

Spring of 2004, my mother hasn't spoken to me since our scene in Times Square. On her birthday, March 24, I send her flowers. We resume our relationship as if nothing has happened. We do this. Crisis, fighting, accusations, swearing at each other, not speaking for weeks or months—or in one case, Nena and Pepin spent five years not speaking to each other. I know that like her son, Nena has an internal rage, and I am convinced she has voices in her head that lead to the unleashing of the rage. What are they telling her? I think it's the guilt. I think there is an alter ego somewhere inside of her that accuses her and tells her what a terrible person she is. When there is a "safe" person with whom she can unleash the anger, the willing victim becomes the object onto which these disturbing thoughts and feelings are projected. In October of 2003, I became that person onto whom Nena relieved herself, during that tirade in Times Square in front of my daughter, one of her many irrational explosive moments. My medical training has made me aware for years that Pepin and Nena both suffer from severe mood disorders with delusional, psychotic, paranoid features. They are operating just under the radar for clear detection of their disorder. But it is so obvious once you put together their behavioral patterns.

One of Nena's relatives whom we always knew "something was wrong with" is finally getting psychiatric treatment. After attacking a neighbor whom she was convinced was trying to kill her, a neighbor whom she hardly knew and had been distantly kind to her, that neighbor pressed charges, and the result was the uncovering of this relative's periodic hallucinatory states. I remember when I was eight years old, this person took me shopping for a pair of sneakers. I fell in love with a pair of blue Keds. On our way to pay for them, she stuck her nail into the rim of the rubber surrounding the cloth and was easily able to separate the rubber rim from the cloth. She created a scene in the store. "You people come into our neighborhoods to sell us garbage, but you're not going to take advantage of me!" She turned toward the customers in the store and continued, "People, listen to me! The products being sold here are junk. Don't give these people your money. Let's teach them a lesson . . ." As she became more agitated, the salesman pleaded with her to stop. Some customers were scared, others curious, and others started laughing at her. I was trembling with fear but finally got the courage to quietly beg her to stop. She stared at me as if seeing me for the first time that day, grabbed my hand, and told me how I deserve sneakers from a much better place than this. I never did end up with a pair of sneakers that day.

These patterns of bizarre behavior now had a name, a diagnosis, and therapies to control the symptoms. Interventions are available only to those willing to accept they have a problem, or when there's an episode where the behavior crossed the line by hurting others. My relative in treatment now acknowledges something had been wrong for decades, and through her therapy sessions, she has learned to recognize the early symptoms of when she might be cycling into a manic state of rage or paranoia. "I first feel an immense fury inside of me. Then I cannot sleep. And when I see birds flying into my apartment, I now know how to distinguish if the birds are really there or if they are part of my hallucinations. My psychiatrist then increases the dose of my medications or decides to admit me to the hospital if I feel I cannot control myself" is how she now speaks of her disturbing episodic mental states.

She's doing the work that I pray daily for Nena and Pepin to commit themselves to.

Another phone call.

The phone rings, and Pepin in a barely audible whisper says, "The taunting was the worst. Once she was on the couch with one of her perverts, and I was on the floor staring at the two of them with their arms around each other, dressed and ready to go out. I was begging Mom not to leave us. She slips out of her high heels, points a foot to my face, and tells me she doesn't love me . . . she's laughing, taunting me, and when I start crying, she says that's exactly the reason she's going out tonight, she can't stand my crying . . . she's smiling the whole time she's saying this and leaves the house. When you hear the door slam, you run out to the hallway and, Nelly, you start crying for her. Mama, Ochie, and I try to drag you back in, and you're holding onto the doorknob, yelling for Mom to stay home. Mama keeps reassuring us Mom will be right back, but you insist on holding onto the doorknob. Eventually, Ochie and I start playing Batman and Robin, and you join. But right now, Nelly, forty years later, and her taunting is working me up." I hear the hurt in his voice as he tells me this on the phone.

"Peps, I sent Mom flowers for her birthday, and now we're speaking again. I always forgive her, even though she insists she's done nothing wrong. I feel so sorry for her. That mind of hers is such a burden." I am trying to get him to identify Nena as mentally ill.

"The only way I'll take her in to live with me is if Mom becomes homeless. I have had visions of her as a bag woman on the streets looking through garbage for food to eat. That's where I'll cave in. I wouldn't be able to stand it if I knew she were homeless."

"It's funny you should say this because she's been telling her friends how you've been begging her to come down to Florida to live with you."

"What do you mean? I hardly speak to the woman. She never calls me; I'm the one who always has to call her. When you told me how you're always buying her calling cards, Nell, it hurt me because I thought to myself, *How come she never uses those calling cards to call me?*"

"She never calls me either; she says it's the child's duty to call the parent," I reassure him.

I call my mother after another one of my long, disturbing phone calls with Pepin that are becoming more frequent as we approach May of 2004. "Mom, I think Pepin is in crisis. He's not sounding very well to me, we're speaking to each other more often, and he seems depressed. I keep thinking of his job and how prisoners he has guarded have called his home to tell him they're going to come get him. Mom, do you think something's going on with him? Could he be in danger? Have you heard anything from Niza [Sandra's mother] about how things are going on in his marriage?"

"*Mi hijo esta muy bien* [My son is doing very well]!" she yells back at me. "I speak to him and Sandra on the phone all the time, and they are very happy and *tranquilo*. Don't you start stirring the pot. Leave him alone with his wife. They understand each other . . ." I review these phone calls with my husband, who is also concerned with the depressed tone of my brother's voice, and when I tell him my mother's reaction to my concerns about Pepin, my husband verbalizes this frightening reality: "Nelly, your mother cannot help because she honestly believes that she and her son are talking regularly and that he is well and that he's begging her to come live with him."

Another phone call.

"That bitch sending me to school, smelling like urine, no breakfast. Remember, Nell, when that social worker took you out of class to give us breakfast"? Pepin asks me.

"Yes, she would pull you and me out of class to talk. She loved you," I'm remembering.

"She knew something was wrong, but I couldn't tell her everything. I didn't dare," he says.

"Well, sometimes Mom gave us breakfast," I say, and before I finish my thought, he interrupts.

"Yeah, that ***yema de huevo*** crap." I double over with laughter as he continues to describe the occasional breakfast Nena would make us have when we were children. Carefully she would tap an egg at the edge of the sink. Then peel away a small eggshell crack and let out the white. Once all of the egg white slipped out of the shell, she would gently lift off more of the eggshell so that a quarter-sized opening was made on the tapered end of the egg. She would then fill the egg with Manishchevitz wine and make us drink the wine and raw egg yolk. "That is one crazy woman. I'd get to school, tripping over myself and asking, 'Where's the party?'" He slurs his speech, imitating a drunk person.

I can barely catch my breath I'm laughing so hard. "And the way she'd yell at us to make sure we drank the whole thing," I manage to say.

"Her morning blast—raw egg yolk, shot of wine. Way to start your morning." He's maintained his composure without breaking out into laughter, which is what makes him so funny. He reminds me of Spaulding Gray in *Swimming to Cambodia,* how he matter of factly describes outrageous scenes that occurred with a sense of irony that is not calculated, just the facts.

Another night, I'm falling asleep, and the phone rings.

"Nell." Pepin is barely audible. "How are the kiddies?"

"Fine, they're asleep." I feel his pain as if transmitted to me via the phone cables, and the depression engulfs us both. "How are Christina and Sandra?"

"Same old shit over here. Sometimes I wish a bomb would go off in this place just so the people here in Miami could refocus on more important things like why corrupt development is allowed to continue choking us off with pollution. You know, I have become aware of so many things working in the federal prison. Nell, so much is going on. I just can't give you the details. I don't know if the phones are bugged, but there's some serious stuff that's coming down the pikes. Armageddon is right around the corner. The days of the empire are numbered. Every empire comes to an end . . . The government is afraid of everything he knows, so they let him have his mistresses and live up the life even though he's supposedly in custody."

"Who?" I ask, as he sometimes talks of others as if I knew who they were.

"That drug-dealing bastard from Panama—Noriega," Pepin answers. "Man, Nelly, if the American public knew half of what's going down, people would be building bunkers in their backyards to prepare. Not here. We're only inches above water. These plywood houses they build down here are on toxic landfill. When I dug a hole in the ground to put in my mailbox by the curb, after just a few shovels, I could see the ocean beneath the ground. It reminds me of what Mom said about the houses down here. '*Es que estas casas estan hecha de carton* [These houses down here are made of carton].'" He's laughing now. "You know, I have a theory about Mom and her whole lunatic family. They were taken out of their natural environment, and their behavior was just not adaptable to New York City. They should've all stayed in that jungle where they came from. The amount of money that family has cost the US government in Welfare, Medicaid, Food Stamps, Incarceration, damn, it's unbelievable. Remember, Nells, when we'd be walking down the street, and she'd yell, 'Nelita, Pepin, *tengo que mear*,' and she would squat between two parked cars to pee. I blocked the traffic side and you the sidewalk until she finished her business. I told that savage one day, 'You hold your urine till we get home. Pee in a toilet like a normal person.'"

At this point, I could not contain my laughter, even though I know he was not intending to be funny. "I think this is the first case of a child toilet-training their parent," I said, cracking up.

"I could still feel the embarrassment when Mom would send me to buy the big purple box of Kotex maxi pads with the fake money coupons from back in the day, and the supermarket clerk would tell me I could only buy food with them shits. Eventually, I learned to buy them from the Bodega. Then there was never a paper bag big enough to cover what I was carrying, so walking back through the block, my friends all laughed as they saw that all too familiar packaging for the woman's time of the month. Finally one day, I told her, 'No way. You know you're gonna get your period. Why the fuck do you wait till the last minute to send me out to buy them shits for you? Get your own Kotex.' Imagine that, Nelly, I'm about ten years old and having this argument with her." As I listen to him, I remember the little, blond head carrying the brown paper bag with the edge of the purple box sticking out and trying to hide his head from our friends. I'm remembering waiting to go to the supermarket with the food coupons, waiting to make sure no one we knew saw us paying with the food stamps. I remember when the cashier would rip out the pastel paper from the booklet, that looked like Monopoly money and sometimes holding it up to make sure it wasn't fake. I remember loving that we got real money for change sometimes and hit the five-cent machines for the fake jewelry that came in the clear plastic bubbles. I'm smiling to myself, and such reminiscences make me chuckle even though I know Pepin is not at all trying to be funny. Even in his deeply depressed states, the way he tells a story just cracks me up. Just like our mother.

"Peps, did you ever think of confronting Mom about these toxic feelings that keep churning inside of you? First I would see a therapist about how to proceed, but instead of allowing this rage to take over, my love, put this to rest," I plead with him.

"Yeah, Nells, I do, but then I say to myself, she's old and going to die soon. But yeah, I do think about driving up there and doing just that. Then I think it will end up with me stabbing her or choking her once she starts denying what a whore she was. And then I say to myself, what the hell, I'll drive up there, get it over with, drive back to Miami, and no one will ever know it was me." He's crying.

"Peps, are you really fantasizing about killing your mother?" I ask.

"Just when she starts in on me. She can still make me crazy, especially when she goes off, putting me down about the fact that

I should have finished high school, how she had to constantly do laundry, washing the sheets I urinated on until I was a teenager, all her disappointments in me whenever I try to bring up something from our past that she did. Then, Nells, yes, I get those thoughts. That's why I stay away from her," he reassures me.

"Well, I did confront her about ten years ago when we first moved into this home. She was visiting frequently to see my children, which also meant I had to deal with her occasional outbursts. One day, she was quietly cooking in my kitchen when all of a sudden I hear her scream. '*Coño, Morton Salt, carajo Nelita, tu sabes que yo solamente uso Diamond Cristal salt*.'" Her yelling escalated, repeating how she cannot cook with Morton salt since the measurements are different than what she is used to, and now her food is not going to taste good. Peps, that woman would not shut up. She kept getting louder and louder and then started throwing utensils around the kitchen when I finally had to step in and yell at her to be quiet. We yelled at each other when I had to tell her to leave, that I didn't want my kids to witness this. She pointed her finger at me and said God was going to punish me for disrespecting my mother. That pointed finger just set me off, Peps. I told her this is the reason we can't have her over to participate in our lives and be part of our families. I told her that if God is going to punish anyone, it will be her for the despicable way she behaved when we were children, especially with those men she would bring home. She covered her ears and started screaming that she does not want to hear this. She said something, Peps, that shocked me. With her palms covering her ears, she yelled back, 'Let me die without ever hearing this . . . 'I told her she needs to get down on her knees and ask for Pepin's forgiveness, that maybe then he will start the path toward peace. She ran out of the house, followed by another few months of us not talking to each other until I finally reached out to her." What I did not tell Pepin about this day is that Nena had answered me that the one who needs to get down on his knees and ask for forgiveness is Pepin for the trouble he put his mother through. I knew this would trigger Pepin's rage, so I did not repeat it.

What I also did not tell Pepin was that during that confrontation with Nena, I said to her, "You're always saying that you don't know why Pepin hits his wife, since he never saw a man hit you. Well, Mom, there are other reasons little boys can grow up with rage against women. Mothers who betray them, whoring with different men right in front of their faces."

Not all our phone calls were this charged or dark. We did laugh and reminisce many times over events in our lives. But these calls where he was filled with rage or depression worried and scared me, and I feared for what my brother could be capable of.

May 2004

"*Brown v. Board of Education*—Where Are We Today?" is the title of the conference here at the Apollo Theatre in Harlem that I am attending with my daughter, Sarah. My good friend and champion in the cause to enlighten us all regarding inequalities in our society, the author Ellis Cose, is moderating this panel discussion. Most of us in the audience are united in our unsettled relationship with an educational system where apparently bright, young people, who happen to be poor, have so much trouble succeeding in. What will it take to give a young child who comes to school hungry, distracted by trauma and a short attention span, and with no one at home to help with schoolwork—what will it take to turn them into successful, self-realized human beings to the benefit of us all?

I have finished reading *One Mind at a Time* and am learning that different kinds of thinkers with their own unique strengths are finally being recognized, and the education community is moving toward tailoring curriculum to fit our divergent thinkers. I have read all of Jonathan Kozol's books, this man who feels the pain of the muted voice of a child misunderstood and who has methodically shown us through the last four decades of his writings how our public education system gives the least to those who should get the most in funding. Give poor children an equal playing field. I have had the privilege to have gotten to know people, such as my teachers at Aquinas and Dr. Harriet McGurk, my clinical instructor during my time at Columbia Presbyterian Hospital, whose beautiful faces emit love and desire to help all poor children achieve academically. My mind is racing with these ideas where beyond racial desegregation and equal funding for our public schools, we will move toward working with individual differences and center lessons around a mode of instruction that fits each individual's learning style. Too many of our children feel defeated by a sense that they cannot reach their potential and therefore turn away from their educational institutions toward something else.

I am going to write my own book, *Divergent Thinkers*. Ideas are swirling through my mind as I begin to hone in on the key to unlock the mystery of why so many of our underprivileged children give up on their dreams, sometime in early adolescence. That transition between middle and high school is where so many of these souls get lost. My book will center around the four of us—Gilbert, Pepin, Ochie, and me. My hope is that this book will answer the question so many people throughout my life ask me, "Why did you make it and not them?"

Pepin, always at the top of his class in grammar school but with a tendency to drift away from his lessons to concentrate on his drawings in the middle of a class day. He was a talented artist and would fill composition books of portraits, especially that of naked ladies. Although he would of course get into trouble for this, no one could put down his artwork without commenting on the superb technique. I don't think he's picked up a crayon to draw in twenty-five years, a sad note in explaining how creativity is many times beaten out of our children as they go through the educational process. What are Pepin's educational needs that went unaddressed for so many years, which led to this very bright, young man dropping out of high school? What are his psychiatric needs that have gone untreated for so long, the ones that have led to his recurring cycles of violence interspersed with depressive states?

Ochie was to be another one of my subjects to receive a full neuropsychiatric evaluation to see exactly what his strengths and weaknesses are. To see how we could've helped him achieve his goals. To look at what we learn from his story so as to prevent others from following in his path. He recently got out of prison, having finished another three-year sentence. He has spent more time in jail since the age of twelve than free. He's just turned forty, and maybe we will finally uncover the answer as to why Ochie dropped out of school in sixth grade and found his place in the world of crime.

Gilbert, now dead for three years. A comedian with such a quick wit. I remember when I was in fifth grade, 1972, I wore the same shirt every day. The shirt had rows of cats patterned on it, and it acquired the smell of urine from Pepin's bedwetting. One day, Gilbert said to me, "Nelly, it's time to change that shirt. Those cats are saying, 'Meow, *meao.*" (A play on words as urine in Spanish is also *meao.*) He was our very own Richard Pryor. So what was his reason for not getting beyond the ninth grade? He also had that rage that periodically exploded. What more could society have done for him as a child to prevent an obviously bright student from becoming addicted to heroin for thirty years and spending countless days hanging out in front of the "OTB" in the bus station of 178th Street? Although we could no longer study his psychological patterns and needs, his letters written while in rehabilitation might give us some clues.

In thinking of these boys, in looking for the clues that would uncover their psychological burdens that impaired their abilities to learn and therefore succeed in school, I hypothesized in this book I began to write that we could then not only find the way to accommodate their divergent minds in our current educational system, but also see their school failing as a symptom that would lead to further psychiatric evaluation and treatment to prevent their underlying mental illnesses from worsening.

And then to answer the question as to why I was able to succeed despite the fact that I knew I wasn't the smartest of this group would reveal the fact that I also was probably the least creative. I was able to regurgitate the information fed to me precisely as was asked for during a test. I also knew within me that a driving force for success was my need to block out all that had happened. As a child, I became detached from the strong pull toward engaging in the endless fighting between Nena and my brothers. I escaped into books and dreamed everyday of a future away from that home. As I got older, I also did not relive these early childhood experiences the way the boys did; they never seemed to get over early childhood trauma. I didn't have a learning disability that impaired my success in school. I was given the gift of idealism, which I know is a characteristic of resilience in children. I believed that I could make a difference. I was going to "save" those poor children who impacted me so deeply on my first visit to the Dominican Republic. I was also going to solve this problem of the young people in our community who just simply give up and turn to the streets.

I was so hopeful that my book would bring healing to so many who have felt completely demoralized at having failed at school and therefore at life. After the conference, surrounded by these great minds who have served on the panel discussion, we shared our ideas over dinner.

"We should create a school where different classrooms will accommodate students who need a different approach to learning, the auditory learner, the child whose style would benefit more with experiential learning, etc. We should give the first opportunity for these accommodating schools to our most vulnerable children, those in foster care. They deserve the best educational system our country can provide. These are the wards of the state; thereby they are our children. If we do this for them, they will become our future doctors, teachers, and leaders. We should be pouring money into making every aspect of their lives filled with the opportunities that the children of the privileged have. Instead, we allow them to go from home to home, transferring from one poorly performing school to another, and risk the poor outcomes they have later in life that we see too often." I say this to Ellis Cose, his wife, Lee Llambelis, as well as the others present.

"Although what you say is logical and the right thing to do, we live in a society where the taxpayer doesn't want to pay for someone else's child," Ellis says.

"But we do pay, by allowing them to fail out of school, by not giving them the proper medical attention, by not supporting their mental health needs; we pay the price by allowing some of them to enter into the criminal world," I say to this couple who is ahead of me in fighting for social justice. Incarceration is so much more expensive in terms of real dollars than education. Yet punishment always seems more attractive to voters than providing preventative services.

Mother's Day 2004, the phone rings. "Hi, Nanny. Happy Mother's Day." It's my niece, Christina, calling me from her cell phone while she drives.

"Mamita, thank you for calling me. It makes me so happy to hear from you, but please don't drive and talk on the cell phone at the same time" was my answer.

"It's okay, Nanny. I have a headset on," she reassures me.

"How are things at home? I haven't heard from your father." It usually means he's back together with Sandra and is too embarrassed to admit this to me, so the phone calls from him are less frequent, but I don't say this to her.

"Very tense, Nanny. I finally came to the conclusion they need to get a divorce. It's the right thing. I always wanted my family to stay together, but I'm so tired of it all, it's time for them to go their separate ways." She is logical, she is right.

"And what about you? Why don't you leave the house and come live with me or at the college dorm/"

"I don't want to leave my mom alone with him."

My all too familiar sick-to-my-stomach feeling has started upon hearing these words. The images of my brother beating on his wife, although I've never actually seen it happen, pop up vividly and fill me with fear and disgust.

"Nanny, my dad plans to go visit you on Memorial Day weekend."

"Really? He swore he'd never come to New York again, and now after fourteen years, he's visiting? I'm thrilled he's coming, but why?"

"I don't know, but he wants to come up. He wants me to go with him, but I have to see if I can take time off from work." She's relieved Pepin is reaching out to me. They know the calming effect I have on him.

"Christina, I'm going to call your dad right now so we can start planning his trip. I love you, and, Christina, please understand you are not to blame for the insane relationship your mother and father have." I say this in response to her previous statements to me, that she knows she's been the cause of her mother's misery. She has also told me in the past, "Nanny, I'm just like him. I'm just like him, and it scares me." I would always answer, "No, Christina, you are just caught up in an insane situation, but you are not like your father." I then repeat to her the lesson taught to me at Aquinas High School: "Christina, we come through our families, but we are not destined to become them. What we can do is learn from our circumstances how to make life better, more peaceful for ourselves and others." And so before hanging up, I reassure her she has loving kindness in her heart. It breaks my heart and fills me with guilt to know what she has witnessed between her parents.

Pepin and Nelita on the Deck

The Last Picture of
Pepin and Nelita
May 30, 2004

Pepin Waving Good-bye

May 30, 2004. Pepin and Nena slept over at my house. The three of us together in New York, something we thought would never happen again. When Pepin moved out of Washington Heights in the late eighties, he said, "Nells, I've got to leave this place. Everywhere I look, my friends look like zombies from *Night of the Living Dead*. Sometimes I do a double take when I see a buddy still alive, that empty look in their eyes, when they're high. Seems like everyone is just shuffling along looking for their next hit of crack or marijuana or heroin." He repeats this now. He seems to be drifting in his conversation between the past and today.

"Like Ochie, Nells, I think about him all the time. I look him up in the database at work and always know when he's locked up again. It's a knife in my heart when I think of him. I still feel guilty about giving up on him. But when I gave him that job in housekeeping and he kept coming into work late and high, thinking he could get away with it because I was his boss, well, I couldn't have it. When I fired him, I told him I loved him as much as I love Nelita, but I couldn't see him all fucked up anymore, it was killing me. We hugged and cried, and he gave me all the sob stories these drug addicts always give. Talking about his father abandoning him, and his mother verbally abusing him and not giving him any love, how he tried to concentrate in school but couldn't. I just couldn't listen to that bullshit anymore.

"I also felt back then that if I stayed in New York, Nells, I was going to kill somebody. This crack epidemic was making everyone so violent. Anarchy had taken over, and these crackheads were willing to shoot you dead over a parking spot or a gold chain around your neck. I had to get out for my daughter's sake."

So after fourteen years, Pepin decides to visit New York, and today is our last full day together, Sunday of Memorial Day Weekend in 2004. This visit has been wonderful. Pepin and I have laughed so much, reminiscing about our childhood and especially the teenage years, the disco years, and all the clubs we would go dancing in. Back then, there was no such thing as proofing us at the door of a nightclub, and we'd spend all night with our friends doing the hustle at Ipanema, Roseland, Starship Enterprise, and illegal dance clubs in the Bronx, Washington Heights, and Harlem. On summer nights, Peps would set up his DJ equipment outside in Cabrini Park, spin his records, and we'd party until the cops came to make us turn the music off. We walked around the old neighborhood, P.S. 173, Jayhood Right Park, retelling stories of his wildness, including tearing down the Henry Hudson Parkway on his motorcycle without a helmet going a hundred miles an hour. He points to the George

Washington Bridge and remembers the time when he was four years old and decided to walk across it by himself.

"Yes, Peps, I remember the cops at the house, Mom and Pops sitting on the sofa, and you in the arms of one of the officers. How in the world did you get from our apartment on 169th Street all the way onto the bridge? I mean, it's hard for an adult to find the pedestrian entrance," I say.

"I just knew, but where the fuck was our mother that I was just able to walk out of the apartment? You know, that's the same ramp where Gilbert used to throw bricks at cars driving onto the bridge. Crazy mother fucker. But shit, Nena destroyed him too," he says in a sad tone.

That weekend, we walked around Ground Zero where he worked as a janitor, in one of the twin towers, in the 1980's. We went to Chinatown to eat. Every nightclub we used to go to no longer existed, and the cleanliness of Manhattan was something he could not get over. We went back uptown to see George Washington High School, from where he dropped out in the tenth grade.

It was a time when the less he went to school, the more I excelled in my studies. While I was saved by Aquinas High School, he went to George Washington High School, which in the seventies was basically just a hang out. One of our neighborhood friends was shot in the back in the school cafeteria and carried the bullet within his body into adulthood. Another neighborhood girl reportedly was raped in the bathroom by a group of girls using a Coca Cola bottle. How many students entering ninth grade at this school during this era actually graduated four years later? Very few, and certainly not my two brothers.

Despite our differences in our educational paths, we always loved going out dancing with our group of friends. My friends at Aquinas all had a crush on Pepin and looked forward to dancing with him on weekends, as he was one of the best hustlers of our group.

These memories of our very different educational experiences left Pepin bitter about his lost potential but always proud that I was safe in my Catholic school and went to college. "I wasn't gonna let you spend one day at George Washington High School. I don't care what I had to do, I wanted to send your ass to Oxford!" he says to me. "Forget Harvard. Oxford for you."

He accompanied me to Montefiore, where I had to round on some patients, and then to my office on the Saturday of that weekend. While there, he asked to borrow my car and returned after a few hours. Earlier that day, we tried to visit Ochie, but after ringing the buzzard to his building with no answer, we gave up. I know Peps really wanted to see him. When he returned, he said he just wanted to keep driving around to see all the old places.

On this beautiful Sunday morning, May 30, 2004, Pepin and I are standing in the backyard of my house in Scarsdale, on the deck. His mood has improved from the very quiet and depressed man I picked up at the airport two days ago, to one who is at least occasionally laughing today. Pepin has on a tight, short-sleeved T-shirt, exposing his bulging muscles, and his dark glasses giving him the look of a bouncer or part of a security detail team. We stand quietly together, and I struggle not to bring up the question of steroid use. So far, our visit has been peaceful, and I don't want to trigger an argument between us. There's always the tension of saying something that might strike him in an offensive way, depending on his mood. I am caught by surprise when I see tears slipping down from under his sunglasses. I cuddle my face in his neck and ask, "Peps, what's the matter?"

"It's her." He points toward my kitchen window where my mother is sitting by herself drinking a cup of *café con leche.* "I hate her so much, I want to snap her neck, and then I say to myself, 'Look at her. She's a pathetic old lady.' What does that say about me? How can I have so much anger toward an old woman like her? Look at her drinking her coffee there helplessly. I want to love her, I want to feel like I should take care of her, and I know I should. I've been thinking of maybe paying some of her bills through my online banking, but then, Nell, I think of how she'd let me go to school smelling like urine," he pulls at his T-shirt, "pee stains on me, and that bitch couldn't get out of bed to help me get ready for school.

The kids would run away from me because I smelled so bad. Here I am six, seven, eight years old, going to school hungry, except for the days when she'd make us take a shot of Manishchevitz wine with the raw egg straight out of the egg shell, couldn't even pour it into a glass." His pain is overwhelming, and I am overcome with so much sadness right now. To be around him when he is like this is to experience what true clinical depression is. So much darkness surrounds him that it engulfs anyone near him. I am literally feeling the temperature drop as a chill runs through me in his presence.

"Pepin, she was sick. I know now she suffered from severe mood disorder. The stretches of mania that made her hypersexual and promiscuous, the irritability where every little thing bothered her, followed by her long stretches of sleeping for days when she would not or could not even get out of her pajamas. Those are all part of a clinical entity that made it impossible to adequately care for us." I hear myself speak and realize I have intermixed myself the doctor into this vulnerable moment for Pepin. However, that is how I deal with this pain. I detach, I analyze, I make it clinical.

"But what does it say about me that all I can think of is physically harming that helpless, little old lady over there? Why can't I just say, 'It's over'?" he says as he clutches his chest, hugging himself.

"It's over, Peps. Now it's time for you and I to enjoy life a little. Do you want me to take Mom home? I've achieved a place psychologically where months go by, and I don't see Mom, and I really don't care to make her a priority. I've put an emotional mile between her and me. I know there can never be the certainty of a rational woman when I visit her, that on any occasion, I don't know what I'm going to get. Will it be the joking, laughing Nena? Will it be the Nena who is ranting about AT&T telemarketers calling her all night long to get her to switch from Verizon? Will it be the Nena who feels maternal today and just wants to come up and cook for me? Will it be the Nena that, upon seeing Morton salt in my cupboard instead of Diamond Crystal salt, will yell bloody murder and throw utensils around my kitchen, followed by a verbal attack on me—about what a terrible daughter I am and how I will be the cause of her stroke because I don't make her a priority in my life? She will create a scene so upsetting in her explosive anger over something as minor as the brand of salt, Pepin, it's exhausting. I can no longer put myself or my family through this. It is not personal, Peps, against you or me—it never was. She just has no insight into her outrageous behavior. And when she is fun and comical and goes out to mingle with people, everyone loves her and cannot see the side that you and Gilbert and I had to endure. So she goes along life not feeling the need to seek mental health; after all, she can be the life of a party, and why would she want to be sedated when she entertains so many people?

"Do you want me to ask her to leave?"

"No, Nell, it's okay. She wants to see her son," he whispers.

My husband has joined us and tells Pepin, "Brother, you are entitled to some happiness in your life. You have to believe that it's okay for you to find peace and some joy. Come stay with us for a while. We're your family too." Jaime puts his arms around Pepin as well. We reassure Pepin that going through a divorce, like he is with Sandra, is traumatic, and he should take time off from work to be with family.

"Peps, if you want to confront her, let's go in a room—you, her, and me—and tell her everything. Let's tell her how we remember everything those perverts did to us, tell her how her constant put downs and the beatings she gave you still hurt you to this day. Tell her about the humiliation, but understand, I have confronted her about all of this already. She will not acknowledge any of it. I once told her that I forgave her for all of this and how much I feel for her pain, having been left alone to raise her children by herself in a foreign country, etc. Her response to me was, 'You are the one that should be begging *me* for forgiveness. I have nothing to regret. I was a good mother who gave you everything, and God will punish you for being such a bad daughter. If I have a stroke and die, it will be because of you.' So many times, especially after I had my children, I wanted to start new and fresh with her, but that ugly monster within her always manages to rear its head. No psychiatrist for her; she insists she doesn't need it."

"It's okay, Nell. I'll be all right. I don't want to deal with any of that. She can hang out with us today." His tone of voice is sounding a little more upbeat. He walks over to the back wall of the house and says, "Nell, you have to get this fixed. You see how the siding doesn't meet the concrete base? That gap will lead to flooding and erosion."

"Always fixing things, you always notice the slightest crack in the wall," I say.

"I can't help it; it bothers me," he says.

"I'll tell Jaime about it. By the way, the beautiful drawing you made of our kitchen, we want you to come back as soon as you can get time off from work and help us redesign the kitchen. I know how much you love home improvement, and you'd be a great help to us."

"Yes, next month I'll come up."

"You promise? I really want you up here. Peps, give me the exact dates so that I can buy your plane tickets. We'll go see the Mets." I repeat, "Peps, you're getting separated from your wife. That's a big trauma. Why don't you ask for a leave of absence from work and spend a few weeks with me here?" I am growing hopeful now that he will allow me to convince him to get into a mental health treatment plan that will allow him to put an end to his anger.

"Baseball, hotdogs, apple pie, and Chevrolet!" we both sing, the jingle Angel Maseda would repeat on our trips to Shea Stadium.

"Peps, please tell me, you are all right. How depressed are you? Do you want to hurt yourself or hurt anyone else? Please be honest with me. I'm worried about you," I say in a tone that makes my panic about his potential for self-harm obvious.

"Look at me, Nells." He curls his biceps and rolls his fingers over his six-pack abdomen muscles. "Do I look like someone who is going to harm himself? Come here, you knuckle head," he says in imitation of Bill Murray during the early years of *Saturday Night Live*. He puts me in a head lock and rubs my skull just like in the signature recurring skit.

In fact, not only did Pepin look great physically, but after those first few hours after arriving, when he seemed so depressed, he was very rational. He talked about the economic impact of the divorce in well-thought-out terms. He told me he had been looking into apartments to move into, since living with a spouse you are divorcing can lead to fighting. He talked about a future where he will find a new life partner and pointed out several women in their twenties he was convinced were giving him the eye. At one point, he said "Shit, look at this body. I'm a get me a twenty-six-year-old wife." Other than obsessively repeating to me that the tire pressure in the wheels of my car was too high, he did not have that constant irritability that can make him so difficult to have around. As I observed this calm in him, I just knew that in my heart once the storm of the divorce was over, he was going to learn to live in peace. He and I were going to have an authentic relationship again where we could talk about our past, and his emotions would be under control.

"Peps, we're just passing through this brief physical existence, my love. Let's make the days between today and our last day as joyful as we can," I said to him in the hopes that he would do as he promised me and see a psychiatrist on a regular basis. I really believed that this time he was ready.

"Okay, we're ready," says my daughter, Sarah. We all pack into our car and head into Manhattan.

Pepin wants to continue visiting all the places he remembers from our childhood and teenage years. While at Times Square, he says, "What the hell is going on here? Where are the peep shows? I mean, I understand we don't want to climb over the hoboes and keep our antennae up for the perverts following little children. But damn, what's Forty-Second Street without a junkie asking you for loose change? This sucks. Pretty soon the whole world is going to look like Disney Land." He seems truly disappointed at how clean this area is.

"UrineTown no more, Peps. Who would have thought back when the city was about to go bankrupt and we thought the Big Apple's days were over as the cultural center of the world, that it would become as clean and safe as it is today?" I say.

Pepin is truly baffled and disappointed that the old, gritty Times Square is no more. He has many moments during this visit where he seems completely lost in thought. Staring, for example, at the East River during our drive into Manhattan, he whispers to himself, "I forgot these were the best years of my life," referring to our teenage years in New York City.

Pepin would also bring up random facts like asking my mother, "Why was it that when we got sick, instead of taking us to the doctor, you called Rosalina to come over and give us a *despojo*? We'd be burning with fever and coughing our heads off, and there she comes with her blue and red scarves, singing her incantations that always ended with *sicaria* and blowing cigar smoke in our faces while she called on the spirits to heal us. Damn, Ma, last thing we needed was someone puffing a Cuban cigar at us." And with these descriptions, he would have us laughing so hard I literally had tears coming down my face.

Nena grabs Pepin by the waist and starts kissing him. "*Mijo, tu sí sabes hacerme reír,*" she laughs, remembering her reliance on the *espiritistas y curanderas* from our neighborhood to cure everything from the common cold to the recovery of the lover you recently lost.

Sunday afternoon, Pepin is looking at Jets jerseys when Lisa, Neida's daughter, calls me. "Nelita, Ochie's dead, we don't know what happened. Mommy just went to wake him up, and he's dead."

"Lisa, we're coming right over." I yell inside the store, "Peps, Ochie's dead!" and we run toward the A train to Neida's apartment on 174th Street. My kids, husband, and mom had already left in the car since they were tired of walking around, and Pepin wanted to continue visiting places with me.

"Peps, here you are after fourteen years, and what kind of a sick coincidence is it that Ochie should die today—today when you are here? Why didn't we go see him together yesterday . . ." I am going on and on incredulously during this train ride. I'm in shock, crying, and feeling regret that I had not seen Ochie in a long while. But

Pepin, he seems so calm. No, he actually is perking up, becoming animated, and is surprised to see tears running down my face.

"He did it because of me," Pepin says.

"What? You mean when we looked up at his window when we could not get into his building, he was looking back at us? You think that little rejection of not going upstairs to see him made him kill himself? Well, you may be right. When you're suicidal, a small gesture like that could be the last straw." I am making assumptions to justify my guilt that I did not make more of an effort to see Ochie. The pain of this loss now has me sobbing, so Pepin puts my head against his chest. He's telling me that Ochie is in a better place, that his life as a drug addict in and out of jail was no life at all.

"Finally he's resting, Nells, like Gilbert. It's over, and we can all have some peace," he says, trying to comfort me.

The Incident

Wednesday, June 9, 2004. I am making coffee. It's about 5:30 in the morning when the house phone rings. I jump to answer it since I don't want my kids to wake up yet. I am also startled because of the hour in which this call is being made. "Hello," I answer.

"She's making me feel guilty," I can barely hear Pepin say. I know this tone of voice; he's depressed. When in this state, he speaks in a barely audible whisper. His state of mind in turn makes me anxious.

"Pepin, you're still sharing the house with her? This is not a good idea. Come up to New York right away. I'll buy the airline ticket right now." My voice is becoming agitated. I have to suppress my hyper alert tone because it will make him withdraw. He is always so careful not to agitate me, not to give me more problems.

"I can't take time off from work right now," he answers very slowly, with long pauses between each word.

"Peps, where are you right now?"

"Driving to work." I feel relieved that he is going to the place he tells me repeatedly he loves, his job. That relieves me since I know he will be around others soon. We remain on the phone about an hour. I do most of the talking.

My lecture to him includes me saying, "It's time to deal with your past, Pepin, to put it to rest so that you can live the rest of your life with some peace . . . Why can't you just tell Sandra how wrong you were with whatever specific instances she is bringing up and let it go? You don't have to win the next argument . . . Christina is an adult now, you will not lose her, she will always be your daughter, she'll just visit her parents in two different places . . . You worked hard and sacrificed to give your family a nice life, take credit for it . . . Pepin, did you ever think how much I need you? You who protected me, who took hits from the thugs and perverts in the neighborhood to make sure your little sister went unharmed, I miss you, my love. I want you here in New York . . . I know what Nena did to us. What she let her boyfriends do to us is something that is simmering in you, Peps, but trust me, that anger can be conquered. I did it in therapy, and now I just feel sorry for her. For example, that almost daily rant about not ever wanting us, that we were conceived during a time of unreliable contraception and so on, well Peps, instead of making me angry that she would say such horrible things, I actually feel sorry for her. Not only because she is obviously not in a right mind, but because despite not planning for us and not wanting children, she stuck by us, gave us a roof . . . Peps, how is Christina?"

"She's beautiful. We're just not getting along right now. Nelly, I'm at work, I have to hang up. I love you," and we hang up.

I cannot stop thinking about Peps. I alternate between worrying about him harming himself and feeling anger that this cycle in his marriage continues. One day they are getting separated; the next day they're together; the day after that, Sandra is knocking on my cousin's door, crying, asking that she be allowed to stay there for a few days since Pepin is "going berserk"; then they're seen hugging, kissing, and laughing as though they're newlyweds. The truth is, it seems that everyone who is a friend or relative of this couple has just about had it with their ups and downs over the last twenty years.

So many times, Nena has said, *"Ya yo no encuentro ní las palabras con que hablarle a Sandra.* I'm tired of telling her to leave Pepin, that she is going to bring about a tragedy by staying with him. She does not listen, always goes back to him for more. I'm tired of those two." And although I feel the same weariness, today, after this phone call, my mind is continuously thinking and remembering and preparing that speech that will finally get through to Pepin and magically give him insight and rational thought regarding what he needs to do. I call him back after a few hours, and we talk during his lunch break.

"Peps, how is the day going? Have you thought about what I said?" I ask.

"Nell, I'm fine, stop worrying. It's normal for someone to be depressed while going through a divorce. I am not going to do anything crazy. I'm seeing a psychiatrist, and he has me taking Lexapro, which really helps. In addition, when I get agitated or get what I think are panic attacks, I take a Xanax to chill me out. By the way, I can't go to New York until July." His voice remains monotonous, but still, he seems rational, which calms me.

"Oh, by the way, a friend offered me free Met's tickets for the weekend of July 17, so now you have to come," I say, as I have given up on getting him to New York immediately.

"I love you, Nells. You've made me so proud," he says, and then he tells me he's got to go.

"I love you so much, Peps. I've missed you. I can't wait until you come up to New York again." I really mean what I say; I miss my lovely brother who is always watching out for me. Later that day, I tried calling him back several times but did not get to reach him.

I wrote him an e-mail on June 9, 2004 at 9:39 p.m., and on the subject line, I wrote, *How are things?* The e-mail said, *Is everything going all right? I'll call you over the weekend.*

Love, Nelly.

Pepin had written me some e-mails before this day that substantiated what he said about being in therapy and served to reassure me he was getting the mental health care he needed. They were as follows:

Hi Nell,
For the first time, I am a little relieved that I am going to face my ghosts. I would have carried this destruction wherever, and with whomever I was with. In order for people around me to be better, I first have to be better myself. I am talking to Christina every day. She appears to be eager concerning therapy. Will call this weekend.
Love,
Pep

*   *   *

I'm okay. Communication lines between Christina and I have reopened the last two days. We are going to try family counseling in three weeks. We had the first heart to heart. She's a very angry young lady with some valid points. I have been somewhat in denial of the problems that plague me. I am going to face my problems once and for all. It's the only way that I am going to survive and have some peace in my life.
How are the kiddies?
Love,
Pep

June 12, 2004 is a very warm, sunny day in New York. I'm up early on this Saturday morning because I have patients scheduled in my office. As I make coffee quietly in order not to wake the others, I realize how tired I am. I had a hard time sleeping last night, though I'm not sure why. I was agitated, woke up several times, and had difficulty getting back to sleep. Last night, I hung out with my dear friend Lee, and I spent most of the evening ranting to her about my brother Pepin. At one point while I drove her back home to Manhattan, I was practically yelling, "Those two keep getting back together, and what am I supposed to do? Nothing, just listen to the back and forth between those two. You know what I told him, Lee? I told him if they have some kind of perversion going on—you know, some kind of sadomasochism freakiness—that they need to keep it in their bedroom and not involve other people, like my cousins who keep taking Sandra in for a day or two when Sandra claims to be leaving Pepin, only to watch her go back . . ." I went on and on. I was still feeling this anger, agitation, and worry this morning because I have not heard from Pepin since Wednesday, which meant that his relationship with Sandra was back on. He was therefore too embarrassed to call me, given how much we have recently been talking about his divorce, I assumed.

As I'm walking into my office, my cell phone rings, and I see it's a call from Christina. *They probably had an argument again*, I think to myself as I answer the phone. Still, I realize, it's a little too early for one of these all too familiar phone calls. Instead of Christina, it's a man's voice. "Nelita, it's Ray, your brother's neighbor. Are you sitting down?"

"What happened? What happened? What happened?" I am screaming those same two words over and over again. In the background, I hear hysterical voices.

"The police have told me not to say anything over the phone, Nelita. Christina needs you," he says.

"How can you call me and not tell me what happened? Where's Christina? Is she okay? Tell me what happened!" I shriek.

"Christina is in shock, but she's physically okay." I can tell Ray is crying, and in the background, someone is also crying that they want their mommy.

My call waiting beeps, and I click over to the other call.

"Nelly, it's Manchi [a relative who lives in Miami]. *Ay que tragedia.*" He's crying.

"What happened? No one is telling me what happened!" I yell.

"Your brother shot Sandra and then shot himself."

I run to my car, cell phone by my ear, and tear down the highway, zigzagging in and out of traffic. I tell Manchi, "Let Christina know I am on my way to the airport. I'll be in Miami as fast as I can go." I call my cousin Alfy (Ochie's younger brother) and say, "Pepin shot Sandra and shot himself, Alfy. I can't tell Nena. I cannot be the one to tell her. Please go over there," I plead with him.

"Want me to come to Miami with you? Damn, first Ochie, then Pepin—damn, this can't be happening. Nelly, this can't be a coincidence, I can't believe this." He starts crying.

I have to listen to what people that I'm calling are telling me. I need to slow down, drive carefully, and stop talking on the phone. But as soon as I get off the phone, the grief swells, and I start punching the steering wheel and howling in pain, "Why, why, why?"

155

Federal Correctional Officer shoots wife, turns gun on himself

Officer shoots wife, turns gun on himself

From Sunday's *Miami Herald* June 13, 2004

A **corrections officer** fatally shot his wife before turning the gun on himself in the couple's Country Walk home early Saturday, Miami-Dade police said. The bodies of **corrections Officer** Jose Maseda and his wife, Sandra, were found by their 19-year-old daughter in the master bedroom. Family members told police the couple had been having marital problems for "quite some time," according to a police report. People who live in the neighborhood, many of whom also work in law enforcement, were stunned by the events. "We live in a quiet neighborhood and we have never had trouble in the 10 years I've lived here," said Zoraida Ramos, 41. "We are surprised to hear about a tragedy of this magnitude." Neighbors gathered on their lawns Saturday as authorities investigated. A Miami-Dade police report said the couple died from "apparent gunshot wounds." It added: "Investigators believe it was a **homicide/suicide**." Sandra Maseda was listed as the victim in the shootings. Neighbors said she had temporarily separated from her husband months ago, but the couple had recently been spending time together again. Neighbors said Jose Maseda was a **federal corrections officer**, but did not say where. They said several **federal vehicles** were parked outside the house after the shootings.

The detectives recreated the scene and this is what I know of that fatal day. Christina awoke to find her father sitting in the kitchen, staring into space, not responding to her questions, not talking at all. Christina, although disturbed to see him this way, did what her mother had taught her to do during these episodes of Pepin's. She showered him with affection in hopes to, in her words, "Get him out of his depression." She states that although it scared her to see him this way, and she wanted to stay, she needed to get to school and knew her mother would take care of him, so she left. Later that day, Sandra and Pepin went out, bought a quart of vodka, and rented a movie. Both drank heavily that Friday, June 11, 2004. Christina says that evening they argued because Pepin wanted to share dinner and a movie with her, but she refused and left to be with her friend. Apparently, that argument continued between him and Sandra. Their last argument. He shot his gun at her five times, most of the bullets centered right on the chest wall area over the heart. Pepin then wrote a note on a scrap piece of paper: *I just can't take it anymore.*

He then took the portrait of Angel Maseda, hugged it (and/or spoke to it, the detectives surmised), put that picture of our father face down on his bedroom bureau, put the gun in his mouth, and shot himself.

The following are things people said at the funeral.

"Nelita, we tried everything to get Sandra to leave," said a friend of Sandra's.

"I had to stop taking Sandra's phone calls because every time she called or came over, hysterical after a beating from Pepin, we would take her in, just to see her go back to him after a few days," said a cousin of mine who lived nearby.

"I want you guys to know that Sandra told me she would never leave Jose, that he was her addiction. She also said that if she could not have him, no one else would," said another friend to Nena and me.

"You are to blame for this. You are his sister and a doctor; you could have avoided this," says an uncle's wife to me, while shaking a finger in my face. Several others over the next few weeks joined in this chorus against me.

At several points, Nena yelled back "**Weetre, todo ustedes.** Anyone who accuses my daughter of any blame is a hoodlum. Yes, my son did the unthinkable, but it is because *she* provoked it." She points at Sandra's dead body while saying this.

And so on went the back and forth of accusations, lamentations, and "I told you so," etc.

Throughout, Niza kept comforting me. "Nelita, *estaban los dos enfermos, ya esto estaba escrito.* Don't pay attention to what any of these ignorant people say. We all knew this day was coming. I miss my Sandrita, but she was not going to leave him."

At the funeral, Niza spoke, "Pray for my daughter, Sandra, and my son-in-law, Jose. I loved them both." For most of us present, this was the most humane act of forgiveness we had ever experienced. Niza *forgave*.

Toward the end of 2004, Nena noticeably changed. Her memory was slipping. She refused to wear anything but black, and when she came out to see people, it was usually because her anger reached a point where she needed to unleash it.

I had her see a wonderful physician at the Neurological Institute of New York Presbyterian Hospital, Dr. Pelton. He confirmed Nena's moderate memory loss, and we put her on a treatment protocol that consisted of an antidepressant and a second medication to improve memory. Nena also developed labile hypertension where her blood pressure would peak to dangerously high levels, causing dizziness and headaches that would land her in the emergency room. Despite the psychiatric drugs having a good effect on Nena's high blood pressure and her mood, she would stop taking them because she "did not want to be a zombie." She felt it took away her "zing." Her siblings encouraged her to stop the medication because "in our family, there are no crazies." Her anxiety and insomnia were helped with Dr. Pelton's prescribed medications, which in turn, along with an anti-hypertensive, helped keep Nena's blood pressure within the normal range. Sometime in late December of 2008, Nena stopped taking these meds. On January 2, 2009, she ended up in the emergency room again, but this time, the findings were ominous. She ruptured her aorta at the level of her renal arties—that is, blood flow from her kidneys and below diminished slowly until it shut down. There was no way to save her.

She had made out her living will, in which she clearly stated that in the event of a terminal event, she wanted nothing done except for palliative medication. She was asked again during this hospitalization, and she looked at me and asked, "*Me llego la hora*[Did my hour come]?"

"*Sí*, Mom. Do you want them to try to save you, maybe with surgery?" I asked.

"No." She waved her hand. "It's over. All I want is for Nelita to stay right by my side."

She remained conscious for over forty hours.

Before she lost consciousness, I asked her, "Mom, is there anything you need to say to me before you leave me?" By then, I had been crying and longing for her. Several times, I buried my face in her neck, telling her how much I loved her and how much I was going to miss her. Now I wanted to know, were there any secrets left untold? I imagined novella-type scenarios, such as, was the man I was told was my father not really my father? What happened to you, Nena, in the Dominican Republic that was such a deep wound you could not talk about it? Can you now tell me, Mommy? What were all those things from your past that you stated 'are all erased'?"

I also wanted her to expand on something I heard her say while we visited Pepin's ashes one day at the cemetery where Gilbert is also buried. During a fit of crying, she stated, "Mijo, I know this happened because of me. I am at fault for what you did." It was shocking for me to hear this since Nena was in constant denial about her role in creating the immense rage Pepin carried. Was she finally going to admit her wrongs to me at this moment? She had already refused to see a priest and confess her sins.

She looked at me, morphine drip going into her veins, fixed my hair, and smiled.

"*Que te quierro mucho* [That I love you very much]," is all she answered.

So many people from Washington Heights came to visit her that hospital security had to be called to try to set order. Her good friend Matias put it best, "*Esa fuerza, esa personalidad unica que nos viene muy poca veces en nuestra vidas* [That unique personality, that strong person who comes into our lives very rarely, will never be forgotten]."

At one in the morning of January 5, 2012, Nena took her last breath while cradled in my arms.

At her funeral, there were hundreds of people, too many to fit in Ortiz Funeral Home. All were telling Nena stories of how she made them laugh, took them in as new immigrants to the various city agencies for services. There were stories about multitude of children she had baptized, her fights with the landlord, her chasing away the drug dealers from the stoop of our building, and so on. There were people present from all walks of life, from Scarsdale millionaires to drug addicts on public assistance, who called Nena their friend.

Exactly one week later, on January 12, 2009, Pepin's first granddaughter, Elizabeth Marley Saavedra, was born to his beloved Christina Maseda.

Epilogue

"Completed suicide occurs in 10%—15% of individuals with Bipolar I Disorder (also known as Manic/Depression). Suicidal ideation and attempts are more likely to occur when the individual is in a depressive or mixed state. Child abuse, spouse abuse, or other violent behavior may occur during severe Manic Episodes or during those with psychotic features. Other associated problems include school truancy, school failure, occupational failure, divorce, or episodic antisocial behavior. Bipolar Disorder is associated with Alcohol and other Substance Use Disorder in many individuals. Individuals with earlier onset of Bipolar I Disorder are more likely to have a history of current alcohol or other substance use problems. Concomitant alcohol and other substance use is associated with an increased number of hospitalizations and a worse course of illness. Other associated mental disorders include Anorexia Nervosa, Bulimia Nervosa, Attention Deficit/Hyperactivity Disorder, Panic Disorder, and Social Phobia."

—From *Diagnostic and Statistical Manual of Mental Disorders, Fourth Edition.*

My twenty-year-old son, Matthew, who is a philosophy major in college (my daughter, Sarah, a graduate of Cornell University, had a very different sojourn to college than mine) and I had a discussion one evening in March of 2012. We were pondering the question of whether or not science will one day make philosophy, the study of human nature, obsolete. This "Hard Consciousness" dilemma, he tells me, centers around the question of what is consciousness? Why do we humans have it? What purpose has it served during our known existence on this planet? Is it a physical entity?

"Mommy, Sartre believed that we are born into this condition. Maybe what you are trying to say is that our human nature is determined by this 'condition' called our bodies, which includes our mind, our brain," says Matthew.

Neuroscience is giving us some clues, at least with respect to what areas of the brain are stimulated by a given stimulant/experience, leading to the release of neurotransmitters, which then leads to our subjective feelings and subsequent reactions. What is the brain? An organ with physiologic functions. An organ that can malfunction like any other. Mental disorders, such as Bipolar Disorder, affect the functioning of the brain the way asthma affects the lungs, or high blood pressure affects the heart.

Genetics show us partially what the inheritance basis is for many of these disorders and elucidate, at the molecular level, its impact on how the brain reacts in certain situations.

Early experiences also determine how our brain's "hard wiring" gets laid down, leading to our life-long action patterns. The following is from developingchild.harvard.edu.

Understanding Intervention

National Scientific Council on the Developing Child
National Forum on Early Childhood Policy and Programs

The future of any society depends on its ability to foster the healthy development of the next generation. Extensive research on the biology of stress now shows that healthy development can be derailed by excessive or prolonged activation of stress response systems in the body (especially the brain), with damaging effects on learning, behavior, and health across the lifespan.

Learning how to cope with adversity is an important part of healthy child development. When we are threatened, our bodies prepare us to respond by increasing our heart rate, blood pressure, and stress hormones, such as cortisol. When a young child's stress response systems are activated within an environment of supportive relationships with adults, these physiological effects are buffered and brought back down to baseline. The result is the development of healthy stress response systems. However, if the stress response is extreme and long-lasting, and buffering relationships are unavailable to the child, the result can be damaged, weakened systems and brain architecture, with lifelong repercussions.

It's important to distinguish among three kinds of responses to stress: *positive*, *tolerable*, and *toxic*. As described below, these three terms refer to the stress response systems' effects on the body, not to the stressful event or experience itself:

Positive stress response is a normal and essential part of healthy development, characterized by brief increases in heart rate and mild elevations in hormone levels. Some situations that might trigger a positive stress response are the first day with a new caregiver or receiving an injected immunization.

Tolerable stress response activates the body's alert systems to a greater degree as a result of more severe, longer-lasting difficulties, such as the loss of a loved one, a natural disaster, or a frightening injury. If the activation is time-limited and buffered by relationships with adults who help the child adapt, the brain and other organs recover from what might otherwise be damaging effects.

Toxic stress response can occur when a child experiences strong, frequent, and/or prolonged adversity—such as physical or emotional abuse, chronic neglect, caregiver substance abuse or mental illness, exposure to violence, and/or the accumulated burdens of family economic hardship—without adequate adult support. This kind of prolonged activation of the stress response systems can disrupt the development of brain architecture and other organ systems, and increase the risk for stress-related disease and cognitive impairment, well into the adult years.

When toxic stress response occurs continually, or is triggered by multiple sources, it can have a cumulative toll on an individual's physical and mental health—for a lifetime. The more adverse experiences in childhood, the greater the likelihood of developmental delays and later health problems, including heart disease, diabetes, substance abuse, and depression. Research also indicates that supportive, responsive relationships with caring adults as early in life as possible can prevent or reverse the damaging effects of toxic stress response.

Questions & Answers

Q: Is all stress damaging?

A: No. The prolonged activation of the body's stress response systems can be damaging, but some stress is a normal part of life. Learning how to cope with stress is an important part of development. We do not need to worry about positive stress, which is short-lived, or tolerable stress, which is more serious but is buffered by supportive relationships. However, the constant activation of the body's stress response systems due to chronic or traumatic experiences in the absence of caring, stable relationships with adults, especially during sensitive periods of early development, can be toxic to brain architecture and other developing organ systems.

Q: What causes stress to become toxic?

A: The terms positive, tolerable, and toxic stress refer to the stress response systems' effects on the body, not to the stressful event itself. Because of the complexity of stress response systems, the three levels are not clinically quantifiable—they are simply a way of categorizing the relative severity of responses to stressful conditions. The extent to which stressful events have lasting adverse effects is determined in part by the individual's biological response (mediated by both genetic predispositions and the availability of supportive relationships that help moderate the stress response), and in part by the duration, intensity, timing, and context of the stressful experience.

Q: What can we do to prevent damage from toxic stress response?
A: The most effective prevention is to reduce exposure of young children to extremely stressful conditions, such as recurrent abuse, chronic neglect, caregiver mental illness or substance abuse, and/or violence or repeated conflict. Programs or services can remediate the conditions or provide stable, buffering relationships with adult caregivers. Research shows that, even under stressful conditions, supportive, responsive relationships with caring adults as early in life as possible can prevent or reverse the damaging effects of toxic stress response.

Q: When should we worry about toxic stress?
A: If at least one parent or caregiver is consistently engaged in a caring, supportive relationship with a young child, most stress responses will be positive or tolerable. For example, there is no evidence that, in a secure and stable home, allowing an infant to cry for 20 to 30 minutes while learning to sleep through the night will elicit a toxic stress response. However, there is ample evidence that chaotic or unstable circumstances, such as placing children in a succession of foster homes or displacement due to economic instability or a natural disaster, can result in a sustained, extreme activation of the stress response system. Stable, loving relationships can buffer against harmful effects by restoring stress response systems to "steady state." When the stressors are severe and long-lasting and adult relationships are unresponsive or inconsistent, it's important for families, friends, and communities to intervene with support, services, and programs that address the source of the stress and the lack of stabilizing relationships in order to protect the child from their damaging effects.

As I have described, Nena's mental state along with the environment of continual crisis had its long-lasting effects on her children. For her boys, who also had the genetic predisposition toward severe mood disorders, this combination was explosive, because they never received the proper mental health-care intervention needed during their childhood. And while I do not excuse in any way what they did, and I believe proper punishment should be the result of criminal behavior, I do think that many of the imponderables, such as "What is the nature of evil?" can find a partial answer in these biochemical changes that occur in our brain. I personally believe that the nature of evil is illness. Simply stated, if you are violent, you need help.

The following is a definition of Mental Disorder. "In DSM-IV, each of the mental disorders is conceptualized as a clinically significant behavioral or psychological syndrome or pattern that occurs in an individual and that is associated with present distress (e.g., a painful symptom) or disability (i.e., impairment in one or more important areas of functioning) or with a significantly increased risk of suffering death, pain, disability, or an important loss of freedom . . . A common misconception is that a classification of mental disorders classifies people, when actually what are being classified are disorders that people have . . . ."

For some children, a parent who is experiencing mentally illness can create an environment of abuse, begetting other ills. Substance abuse, domestic violence, and economic instability are some consequences of this. Children in this environment can experience **emotional abuse,** as in constantly being put down or belittled, **sexual abuse** either by exposure to sexual acts or being used for the sexual pleasure of adults, **physical abuse** by caretakers who do not have the emotional restraint to gently discipline a child, **neglect** of several important domains in life, such as a child being properly clothed and fed, among other forms of abuse.

How do we identify these innocents and intervene in time to safely save not just their bodies, but their minds from continuing in the same destructive paths?

In *Culturally Diverse Children and Adolescents*, Drs. Ian Canino and Jeannette Spurlock write the following about the all too prevalent Post-Traumatic Stress Disorder.

> Post-Traumatic Stress Disorder (PTSD) is characterized by the following symptoms, which occur after the experience of an emotionally disturbing event: reexperiencing the traumatic event, and increased arousal. The initial event may be any one of a broad range of traumas, including natural disasters and those caused by humankind. The witnessing of violence, especially homicide, rape, and suicide, may trigger symptoms of posttraumatic stress disorder. Children uprooted by a natural catastrophe also experience a trauma that may precipitate PTSD. Clinicians should not minimize the untoward effects of parental separation or divorce, neglect, and abuse on children. PTSD can often be accompanied by depression, and there is an increasing body of literature suggesting changes in the hypothalamic-pituitary-adrenal axis and the glucocorticoid levels in the body. Early traumatic experiences may cause prolonged sensitivity to future stress and hyperactivity in the brain regions that contain corticotrophin-releasing factor (CRF) receptors. Because antidepressant drugs reduce the secretion of CRF, they are often used in treating these children with the hope that they will reverse these neurobiological effects (Heit, Graham, & Nemeroff, 1999).

I am idealistic about one day living in a society where we do not indict a child and think of him or her as a criminal just because of the neighborhood and "condition" they happen to be born into. I remember once serving as a chaperone for a school trip my son and his second-grade class were taking to the Bronx Zoo. I sat in the back of the bus with several other mothers and chit chatted about our children. I listened to some of them complain about their nannies, the condition of our tennis courts, etc. As we drove from our very safe and wealthy suburb into the Bronx, some of my neighbors made comments, such as, "Why does the bus have to go through this part of the Bronx where the children have to see these hoodlums?" And, "These people are animals. Look at the garbage on the street." Another said, "I wish the bus would have gone into the zoo directly from the highway. This place is scary. We could get mugged."

As the bus made its way down Southern Boulevard, I asked these ladies to look west on 182nd Street. "See that building with the Spanish tiled roof? That's my old high school, Aquinas, a wonderful school that gave me a great education back in the 1970s. Many of the same teachers I had are still there, and the nuns live in the convent connected to the school. Many of them have lived there for decades serving this community. I love them, which is why I remain active as an alumna of this school and visit as often as I can," I say in a tone that contains my anger. Innocent children live in this neighborhood. Up until the moment when I let everyone know that I too am from here, they had no basis on which to discriminate against me. But that is what some people do with others less fortunate; they dehumanize them in order to make themselves feel separate from "them."

And while neighborhoods, such as those of the South Bronx, are made up mainly of hard-working people who contribute in meaningful ways to our society, areas with high rates of poverty are many times filled with a disproportionate number of people suffering from mental illness. For example, many people with psychological difficulties end up living in homeless shelters. These housing facilities in turn are concentrated in poor neighborhoods, and so we add stressors to local institutions, such as their zoned public schools that further marginalize this population.

It is to our benefit, that we, the "collective we," be mindful of children raised in such circumstances. It does take a village to raise a child. My beautiful friends and neighbors while I was growing up undoubtedly buffered some of the effects of my sometimes hostile and violent home. Rosalina, my obese Cuban next-door neighbor who used to love having me lie on her huge belly while we watched the nightly novellas on Spanish language television. Rosalina, who claimed to be a "medium," a practicing *espiritista*, a different version of Santeria, and used these beliefs to try to help my family. The Archillas who lived on the first floor of our building, always welcomed me to stay at their apartment for as many days as I wanted. They never left me behind when they would go to Harriman Park on Sundays in the summer for a day of swimming and barbecue. My aunt Gabriella who would pick me up, take me to the movies, have me sleep over at her apartment and be the recipient of her need to spoil me.

I am also fully aware that luck played a large role in leading me out of the self-destruction my brothers lived in. My biological endowment did not predispose me to severe mood swings, and I have never had a manic episode the way Pepin would cycle into.

At Aquinas, the teachers pointed me in the direction of a mind that can find fulfillment in a lifetime of learning. But more, they taught me that a life lived in altruistic pursuits is the best method for healing our demons. In fact, the HOPE VI Panel Study "Resilient Children" lists altruism as a characteristic of the resilient child. Those beautiful educators, Sister Margaret Mary, Sister Elizabeth Mclaughlin, Sister Joan Davis, Ms. Magialardi, and Sister Margaret Ryan, were some who greeted me with warmth, affection, and a nice warm Italian roll every morning to get me ready for a day of learning. They were part of the village that helped turn me from following in my brothers' footsteps.

To have a child is an awesome responsibility, a precious gift. Each and every one of us even contemplating taking on this enormous task needs to meditate on the gift and the responsibility and prepare ourselves for it. Trying to raise a happy, well-adjusted child is a goal that is almost impossible to reach, which is why we can only try and learn how to.

It has cost me dearly to have a family that would not submit to psychiatric treatment. So many times over the years, I wondered why Nena never took her boys for mental health-care services when they were young. A large part of the reason is the stigma associated with seeing a psychiatrist—a taboo she just could not overcome, adamantly refusing to have her family labeled as "crazy." But another reason I am certain of is her fear of what they would say about her, about our home life. The shame is not in being labeled; the shame is in not getting the help needed and allowing this violence to continue unchecked. In the Latino community, in general, we do not accept mental health-care services many times because of the social taboo that exists in our culture against being labeled with a psychiatric diagnosis. It is a cultural taboo that too many times leads to tragedy.

After Pepin committed the nightmare of murder/suicide, I began to see a wonderful psychiatrist to whom I am deeply indebted, Dr. Militza Stevanovic. Between my sessions with her and an anti-depressant, I unearthed so much deep and buried trauma that resurfaced after the volcano simmering within Pepin exploded. My grief, my post trauma, my insomnia and anxiety and reactive depression have all been dealt with in this medical context. I continue the work of unshackling myself from the anger, pain, and sadness and every day feel grateful for all the wonderful gifts I have been given in this miracle of life. All that has happened is the drama that I have lived and learned from. It is less anger that fuels my energy, and more love that I feel for "this condition."

I also learned that Pepin lied to me when he told me he was seeing a psychiatrist and taking Lexapro in the days before his horrific crime. And the calm I saw in him, during his last visit, was not because he had sought treatment and was putting his demons to rest. That calm came about because he had made a decision about how he was going to end his life—end it because, as the sentence he wrote before shooting himself stated, "I just can't take it anymore." Tragically, that was not the answer. At that final moment, he did not think about his daughter, Christina, or me, the sister he claimed to love so much. Instead, he created more trauma for all of us who knew and loved Pepin and Sandra.

I feel I am so lucky to be given the gift of a profession where as I heal others, I heal myself. I cannot imagine a greater privilege than serving the beautiful children and their families of the Bronx. Some of them lead lives very similar to mine as a child.

From DSM-IV-TR
Mania
"A manic episode is defined by a distinct period during which there is an abnormally and persistently elevated, expansive, or irritable mood . . . accompanied by at least three additional symptoms that includes inflated self-esteem or grandiosity, decreased need for sleep, pressure of speech, flight of ideas, distractibility, psychomotor agitation . . . Individuals with a Manic Episode frequently do not recognize that they are ill and resist efforts to be treated . . . Mood may shift rapidly to anger or depression."
In Pepin's case, I believe violence against others increased during his episodes of Manic or Hypomanic states.

Depression
"A person is described as depressed, hopeless, discouraged, feeling anxious, irritability, changes in sleep patterns, loss of interest or pleasure, social withdrawal or neglect, changes in appetite, decreased energy, tiredness, sense of worthlessness or guilt, difficulty concentrating. Frequently there may be thoughts of death, suicide ideation, the feeling that others would be better off if the person were dead."

In my dialogues with Pepin, we clearly see many instances of some of these symptoms. It can be seen in what his daughter described about his last full day alive—that he was sitting in a chair, not moving, not responding to others. This may have been a state of catatonia, or at least a severe slow down of psychomotor functions common in depressed people.

Nelly Maseda, MD

Statistics

Suicide is the eleventh leading cause of death in this country among persons aged ten and above. Approximately 34,000 people a year die of documented suicide. **cdc.gov**

Domestic Violence: In 2007, 2349 people in the United States died at the hands of an intimate partner. The National Violence Against Women survey found that 22.1% of women and 7.4% of men experienced physical forms of Intimate Partner Violence at some point in their lives. In the same survey, 7.7% of women or an estimated 201,394 reported being raped by an intimate partner in their lifetime. The medical care, mental health services, and lost productivity (e.g., time away from work) cost of Intimate Partner Violence against women was an estimated $5.8 billion in 1995. Updated to 2003 dollars, that is more than $8.3 billion. **cdc.gov**

According to **Domestic Violence Statistics.org:**

Every nine seconds, a woman in the United States is assaulted or beaten.

Around the world, at least one in every three women has been beaten, coerced into sex, or abused during her lifetime.

Domestic violence is the leading cause of injury to women—more than car accidents, or muggings or rapes combined.

Every day in the United States, more than three women are murdered by their husbands or boyfriends.

Between 55 and 95% of women who have been physically abused by their partners never contacted nongovernmental organizations, shelters, or the police for help.

Depression: In the United States, 9.1% of adults met the criteria for current depression, and 4.1% met the criteria for major depression. **cdc.gov**

Bipolar I Disorder: There are no reports of differential incidence of Bipolar I Disorder based on race or ethnicity . . . In the United States, Bipolar I Disorder is approximately equally common in men and women . . . The lifetime prevalence of Bipolar I Disorder in community samples has varied from 0.4% to 1.6%. **DSM-IV-TR**

Adverse Childhood Experiences (ACE): According to a survey where data was collected between 1995 and 1997, the following percentages were found. Those surveyed were found to have experienced these categories of abuse. **cdc.gov**

Emotional abuse:	13.1% females	7.6% males	10.6% total
Physical abuse:	27% females	29.9% males	28.3% total
Sexual abuse:	24.7% females	16.0% males	20.7% total
Emotional neglect:	16.7%females	12.4% males	14.8% total
Physical neglect:	9.2% females	10.7% males	9.9% total
Mother treated violently:	13.7% females	11.5% males	12.7% total
Household substance abuse:	29.5% females	23.8% males	26.9% total
Household mental illness:	23.3% females	14.8% males	19.4% total
Parental separation or divorce:	24.5% females	21.8% males	23.3% total
Incarcerated household member:	5.2% females	4.1% males	4.7% total

Fatherless Children: According to the US Census Bureau, there are 13.7 million single parents in the United States today. Approximately 26% of children in the United States are raised in single parent homes, and 84% of custodial parents are mothers.

According to Kids Count of the Annie E. Casey Foundation, in 2010, 66% of African American children are being raised in a single-parent home, and 41% of Latino children are being raised in a single-parent home. **cdc.gov**

Mental Health-Care Resources

If you feel that you or someone you know is imminently in danger of a physical threat, please, please, please call 911. From the previous statistics, you see how victims of domestic violence, most of whom are women, rarely access the criminal justice system. Upward of 95 percent never report the battery that occurs in their home.

After Pepin died, I learned from the detective covering the case that the police had gone to their home in the days before this tragedy occurred. When they answered that domestic violence call, they were told by the victim that "it was just a small argument." She refused to follow through with pressing charges.

Many people suffering from violent obsessions psychosis only get recognized after charges have been filed against them, after committing a crime such as battery. And after such attention, their underlying mental health issues are discovered and then hopefully treated. Why was that not done in Pepin's case? Only the victim can proceed with criminal charges. In this case, refraining from pressing charges allowed a violent man to continue hurting others, prevented the receiving of mental health-care that was urgently needed, and finally led to this tragedy. But for me to try to make sense out of why victims of domestic violence fail to call the authorities, or to press charges after the police become involved, is a whole other book in and of itself. The answer is not an easy one or a simple one. Suicide is not the answer.

Pepin and Sandra's nineteen-year-old daughter found her parents' bodies. It is now a trauma she needs to deal with, along with the violence within her home she witnessed prior to this final act.

The human mind is a universe unto itself. If you can identify within yourself any mental strain, such as those described in my vignettes, speak to your doctor about a referral for behavioral health. Most insurance cards have a phone number printed on them with twenty-four-hour access to someone who can point you in the right direction for the help you need.

These services are confidential, and your employer cannot discriminate against you for entering into these categories of treatment.

According to the American Psychiatric Association, "Hispanic Americans use mental health services far less than other racial and ethnic groups."

National Mental Health Association: nmha.org 1-800-273-TALK
National Suicide Prevention Hotline: 1-800-273-8255
National Domestic Violence Hotline: 1-800-799-SAFE

Domestic violence shelters serve women and their children who need to maintain total confidentiality regarding their whereabouts. Your local police precinct can direct you to one of these if you fear for your safety.